W9-AHE-745

COOKIES and SQUARES
with Schmecks Appeal

EDNA STAEBLER

McGraw-Hill Ryerson
Toronto   Montreal

McClelland & Stewart
Toronto

First published in 1990 by

McGraw-Hill Ryerson Limited
330 Progress Avenue
Scarborough, Canada
M1P 2Z5

McClelland & Stewart Limited
481 University Avenue
Suite 900
Toronto, Canada
M5G 2E9

1 2 3 4 5 6 7 8 9 0 W 9 8 7 6 5 4 3 2 1 0
ISBN: 0-7710-8277-0

Canadian Cataloguing in Publication Data
Staebler, Edna, date–
   Cookies and squares with schmecks appeal

(Schmecks appeal cookbook series)
ISBN 0-7710-8277-0

1. Cookies.   2. Baking.   I. Title.   II. Series:
Staebler, Edna, 1906–   .   Schmecks appeal
cookbook series.

TX772.S84 1990   641.8'654   C90-095476-0

Printed and bound in Canada

∞ This book was manufactured using acid-free paper.

CONTENTS

INTRODUCTION

There are no statistics to prove it, but I think the region of Waterloo must be the greatest cookie-baking area in Canada, perhaps in North America, maybe even in the world. All of us natives bake cookies for every occasion or non-occasion. The farmers' wives sell cookies at the markets; so do church groups, Girl Guides, city wives, and bearded young men. There are always big fat cookies — and little fancy ones — for sale at the church bazaars and baking sales, at the Elmira Maple Syrup Festival, at the Wellesley Cheese and Apple Butter Fest, at the New Hamburg Mennonite Sale, and in Oktoberfest beer halls. Kitchener has two cookie factories — Dares Food and Colonial. Every day they sell millions of cookies to stores throughout Canada, the United States, Japan, the Far East, and the Caribbean.

I think my sister Norm makes the best cookies. She has a kitchen drawer full of clippings and hand-written recipes. She always has boxes of cookies stashed away in her cupboard or freezer, and they are consistently neat and delicious. When a recipe calls for shortening, she uses butter. This is her secret: she melts it long enough to come to a bubble, and that gives her cookies a special and superior flavour.

Almost every time I go to Norm's house, she seems to be taking a pan of cookies from the oven. She says, "Oh, kid, try one of these. They're a new kind." But we don't stop at one.

CHRISTMAS COOKIES

When I was newly wed, unconfident, and eager for praise, I'd bake dozens and dozens of cookies at Christmas — nine or ten different kinds of pretty, fussy little things. Then I'd invite friends in to eat and admire them. As I became more experienced and less eager to impress, I baked those that Mother and Daddy made when I was a little girl.

One day in the week before Christmas, Mother would cut up dates, nuts, cherries, and candied peel; we'd have an early supper, clear the big square kitchen table, and from recipes of her grandmother's, Mother would measure out the ingredients and put them into her big blue bowl while Daddy would mix them together. Mother said she needed his muscles to do all the stirring.

When Mother thought the consistency was right, Daddy would roll out the dough. Mother would shape the cookies with fancy cutters and decorate them with red and green sugar or nuts. If I was quiet and good, I was allowed to put the currant buttons and eyes on the gingerbread men and to taste the first cookies that came from the oven, before they sent me happy and dreaming to bed.

SPRINGERLE

It was a Christmas tradition in our family to make springerle (pronounce the *e* on the end). We didn't have the boards that are needed to press down on the dough to emboss the cookies with pretty pictures of birds, animals, and flowers; they always had to be borrowed from the Berner family whose grandparents had brought them from Germany when they emigrated to Kitchener — then called Berlin — long, long ago.

Springerle-making was an exacting procedure: Mother made the dough, Daddy rolled it out and pressed the wooden forms on it, Mother examined the result to make sure the pictures were clear, and then she cut the cookies apart.

I haven't seen a springerle board since I was a child. Now you can buy springerle rolling pins in specialty shops. They work quite well, but I miss a certain little rabbit and the fat dove with the olive twig that were on those old German boards.

4 eggs
2 cups sugar
3½ to 4 cups sifted flour
1 teaspoon baking powder
2 to 3 tablespoons aniseed

Beat the eggs until light; add the sugar gradually and beat until creamy. Beat in the flour and baking powder sifted together, ½ cup at a time, until the dough is of a consistency to roll. On a well-floured surface, roll the dough to a ⅛ inch thickness. Flour the springerle boards or rolling pin and press hard over the dough to leave clear-cut designs. If the dough is too soft, knead in more flour. When you get a good imprint, cut the cookies apart with a knife. Sprinkle buttered cookie sheets with aniseed and arrange the cookies on the sheets. Let them stand uncovered overnight in a dry place at room temperature. Preheat the oven to 300°F and bake the springerle for 15 minutes or until thoroughly dried. They should not be browned, they are virginal — or do I think so because they belonged to my childhood?

LEP COOKIES

There hasn't been a Christmas in my life without Lep Cookies and I hope there never will be. I prefer them to all the rich fancy ones. Mother's recipe, which she got from her grandmother, makes eight cookie jars full; this is only one-quarter of that amount. They can be frozen before or after you bake them.

2 eggs
2 cups molasses
1 cup brown sugar
1 cup sour cream
1 cup almonds, blanched and sliced
   (or 1 cup toasted sunflower seeds)
1 cup chopped citron peel
1 cup chopped mixed peel
1 teaspoon ground cloves
1 teaspoon cinnamon
1 teaspoon aniseed
1 teaspoon baking soda
½ teaspoon nutmeg
7 cups flour

Topping:
Egg white with a bit of water
Whole or split almonds

Stir everything together but the flour. Heat the mixture to lukewarm in a heavy pot or in the top of a double boiler, stirring continuously. When warm but not hot, stir in the flour. Put the mixture in a cool place for a day or two. The dough will then be stiff enough to roll. The ancestral recipe tells you then to roll large spoonfuls of dough until ¼ inch thick with a rolling pin and to cut with a cookie cutter — a hard thing to do because of all the fruit.

Over the years I've found an easier way to make them. I don't know what my great-grandmother would have thought about the short cut, but it certainly suits me, and I think Mother might have welcomed it, too.

Divide the cooled dough into four pieces and roll each piece into a cylinder. Wrap the cylinders in waxed paper and put them in a cold place — or in the freezer — till they are stiff.

When you are ready to bake them, slice the rolls into cookies about ¼ inch thick. Brush the tops with egg white blended with a bit of water, press an almond into the centre of each cookie, and place them on buttered cookie sheets. Bake at 350°F for about 10 minutes.

The Leps will be hard at first. Later they become chewy. They'll keep fresh-tasting long after all the other Christmas cookies have become stale. Once I kept two cylinders in my freezer until the following Christmas — not recommended, but not too bad either. And such a pleasant surprise! I didn't have to stir up Lep Cookies that year.

COMMON SENSE

People using my cookbooks have to use a bit of common sense and initiative. Sometimes my instructions are vague or neglectful. The other day when I was in a shopping mall, a woman stopped and asked if I was who I was. She said she was so glad to meet me because she wanted to ask me about the Lep Cookies in *Food that Really Schmecks*. I had neglected to say that they should be baked. She'd made them and she and her husband had been eating the raw, dried-out dough. They thought they were a bit strange, but they tasted good.

One day before Christmas my niece Mary Lou called me from Toronto. She told me she wanted to make Lep Cookies, which are a tradition in our family.

"Do you bake them, Auntie Ed?" she asked me.

"Of course," I told her.

"But in *Schmecks* you didn't say so."

SUGAR COOKIES

No child should grow up without sugar cookies at Christmas. Mother would cut hers into sheep and rabbits with curranty eyes, Kriss Kringles with tiny red candies for buttons, reindeer, and a man and woman in flat-hatted clerical dress (whose heads and small feet were always bitten off first).

½ cup butter
1 cup sugar
2 eggs, beaten
2 cups flour
3 teaspoons baking powder
½ teaspoon salt
¼ cup milk
½ teaspoon vanilla

Cream butter; add sugar, eggs, and then sifted dry ingredients alternately with milk and vanilla. Roll very thin and cut into fancy shapes — or plainer ones if it isn't Christmas. Decorate. Bake at 350°F till they're pale but done — 10 minutes. Watch! You don't want them to burn after doing all that decorating.

FLOURING COOKIE SHEETS

If you are afraid your cookies might spread or be hard to remove from the pan after they've been baked, try sprinkling flour over the buttered sheet before you place the cookies on it.

ANISEED COOKIES

We children used to call these Annie Seed Cookies and wonder who Annie was. We liked the slightly licorice flavour. Mother said they make best when mixed on a sunny morning.

3 eggs, separated
1 cup icing sugar
1 teaspoon lemon juice
2 cups flour
1 teaspoon baking powder
1½ tablespoons crushed aniseed

Beat the egg yolks until thick, the egg whites until stiff, and combine the two. Gradually fold in the sifted icing sugar and lemon juice. Sift the flour and baking powder and add them and the aniseed to the batter. Drop from a teaspoon about an inch apart on a greased cookie sheet. Let stand on sheets overnight at room temperature. Bake at 325°F until the cookies begin to colour. They'll have a meringue-like top and soft bottom.

GINGERBREAD MEN

How the children love these with their curranty eyes.

⅓ cup butter
⅓ cup brown sugar
1 egg, well beaten
3 cups flour
3 teaspoons baking powder
1 teaspoon ginger
⅓ teaspoon salt
⅔ cups molasses
1 egg white
Currants or raisins

Cream butter and sugar, then add the egg. Sift dry ingredients together and add alternately with the molasses to the first mixture. Roll out until ¼ inch thick. With a small round (shot) glass, cut the head. The body is cut with a glass somewhat larger. Cut the arms and feet with a knife. Join the parts by moistening the edges with egg white and pressing them together to make them stick. Press currants or raisins into the little men for eyes, mouth, and buttons. Bake for 10 minutes at 400°F. Let the children dress up the gingerbread men with frosting if you want them to have some real fun.

PFEFFERNUSSE

These neat little balls are hard as pebbles for the first week. You can't bite them; you just have to suck them or dunk them in coffee as the old-timers do; the dunking gives them a special flavour. They soften with age.

> **2 eggs, separated**
> **1 cup sugar**
> **1 teaspoon cinnamon**
> **½ teaspoon cloves**
> **½ teaspoon white pepper**
> **Grated rind of 1 lemon (optional)**
> **2 cups flour**

Blend the egg yolks and sugar, then fold in the stiffly beaten egg whites. Stir in the spices, pepper, lemon rind, and flour. Mix well and knead slightly on a floured board — the dough is quite stiff. Form into balls, small enough to pop into your mouth. Place them on a greased cookie sheet and let stand overnight to dry. Bake in a 350°F oven for about 15 minutes, but watch them — they shouldn't be brown. If you keep them in a tight container for two or three weeks, they'll soften, but you can hurry the process by putting a quartered apple with them overnight.

MINCEMEAT COOKIES

Because I'm too lazy or too busy at Christmas to make mincemeat, I buy a pint container, which I dilute with a chopped apple when I'm ready to make these cookies or yeast buns.

> **1 cup shortening**
> **1 cup brown sugar**
> **1 teaspoon salt**
> **1 teaspoon vanilla**
> **2 eggs, well beaten**
> **1⅔ cups flour**
> **¾ teaspoon baking soda**
> **2 cups rolled oats**
> **2 cups mincemeat**

Cream together the shortening, brown sugar, salt, and vanilla. Blend in the beaten eggs; sift in the flour and baking soda and mix well. Add the rolled oats and mix thoroughly. Roll the dough to ⅛ inch thick on a floured board, and then cut with a 2½-inch cookie cutter. Place 1 teaspoon mincemeat on a cookie; put another cookie on top and press edges together. Seal all around with a fork. This gives them a crinkly edge. Place carefully on buttered cookie sheets and bake at 350°F for 10 to 15 minutes.

NOËL REFRIGERATOR COOKIES

These are neat, easy to make, and don't need decorating to look festive.

½ cup butter
½ cup shortening
½ cup brown sugar
½ cup white sugar
½ teaspoon lemon extract or juice
½ teaspoon vanilla
1 teaspoon almond extract
2 eggs
2 cups flour
1 teaspoon baking powder
½ teaspoon baking soda
½ teaspoon salt
1½ cups finely chopped, vari-coloured peel

Cream the butter, shortening, sugars, and flavourings until fluffy. Add the eggs and beat them in. Sift in the flour, baking powder, baking soda, and salt, and work them and the peel into the creamed mixture till the dough is smooth. Chill for an hour or so, then shape into rolls and chill again till firm. Cut in ¼-inch slices. Place slices on a lightly buttered cookie sheet. Bake at 375°F for 7 or 8 minutes. Don't let them become brown; they should be pale with all those lovely coloured bits of peel showing through.

MY CHRISTMAS COOKIE PARTY

One year before Christmas I was carried away by so many good cookie recipes that I must have made a thousand! I thought I'd be eating Christmas cookies till Easter since few people venture to my cottage in winter through the winding, snow-blocked lane.

One morning I woke up inspired. I made out a list of people who had invited me to parties or whom I just wanted to see. Then I dashed into town, bought cards that looked like our snowy woods, and wrote, "Put on your boots and come to Sunfish Lake for cookies and coffee any time from nine in the morning till midnight on Boxing Day or New Year's Day." After I mailed them, I counted and found out that I'd invited more than two hundred people! To my little cottage in the country, where any day I might be snowed or iced in!

What if they all came at the same time? How would they navigate our single-track lane lined with swamp and stream? Backing up a half to a third of a mile to let another car pass could mean disaster.

And where would they park their cars? In summer there is room for ten against the rail fence if people are careful. But space for two hundred? There couldn't be. I kept looking at the flat, frozen, snow-covered lake, thinking what a great parking space that would be, but of course there is no way to drive down to it.

Every day for the rest of the week it kept snowing and blowing. I couldn't get in touch with Noah Sauder, the Old Order Mennonite farmer with no telephone who that year was blowing our snow. Maybe the lane would be blocked and no one could get here. But what if they tried and got stuck in a drift? My mother worried, my sister worried, and I worried — I really worried.

Christmas came. Boxing Day came. Noah came early and blew out the snow. Twenty-eight people arrived in the afternoon, ate cookies and cheese, and drank coffee and wine. On New Year's Day the first guests came right after lunch. All afternoon they kept coming and going with such regularity that one would have thought they were scheduled. More than one hundred people drove up the lane, parked their cars, ate cookies, and seemed to enjoy themselves. Only one car got stuck — just when a group was leaving and could give it a shove.

Several enthusiasts suggested that I could have a cookie party every year. "Make it a traditional thing," they said. "It's such fun to come out to this beautiful spot in the country." I agreed. I'd like nothing better than to repeat the performance. Twenty years have passed and I haven't repeated it yet. I remember those awful preliminaries. But every February when I'm still eating left-over Christmas cookies I long to try another cookie party next New Year's Day.

BUTTERSCOTCH BRITTLES

More people asked for this recipe than any other at my Christmas party.

¾ cup shortening (I used chicken fat)
3 cups brown sugar
½ tablespoon baking soda, dissolved in
1 tablespoon warm water
1 cup molasses
3 cups flour
1 cup grated coconut
1 cup chopped walnuts or pecans

Cream the shortening and sugar; add the baking soda and water to the molasses; sift flour and add to the butter mixture alternately with the molasses; stir vigorously. Fold in the coconut and nuts. Let stand overnight in a cold place. Next day, drop by teaspoonfuls on a greased, floured sheet. Bake at 350°F for 10 to 15 minutes.

I hate to tell you this but the first time I tried these they ran together and when I tried to remove them from the pan, they scrunched up into a long narrow blob too hard to bite. For the next panful, I made little balls of the dough, rolled them in flour, and put them far apart on the pans. I had to take them off the pans at just the right moment — not immediately but while they were still hot.

NEW ORLEANS JUMBLES

These look like little Christmas wreaths — with a good flavour.

1 cup shortening
1 cup sugar
Grated rind of 1 orange and 1 lemon or
   ¼ pound mixed, finely chopped peel
3 cups flour
1 egg

Cream shortening, then add sugar and grated rind or chopped peel. Work the flour into the mixture. Break the egg into the dough and work it in thoroughly — sometimes I seem to need 2 eggs. Dredge a board with sugar and on it roll small pieces of dough, as if shaping small bread sticks. Join the ends to make rings about 1½ inches in diameter. Bake on a greased sheet in a 375°F oven until firm but not coloured.

When these are cold, I ice them with a soft white icing to which I add a very, very little bit of green colouring; then I sprinkle them with those tiny multicoloured round candy trimmings to make them look like wreaths.

If you don't want to be so fancy, you can shape the dough into thin cylinders, keep in the fridge for several hours, cut into thin slices, and bake till firm in a 350°F oven.

GOOD OLD-FASHIONED SHORTBREAD

These improve with age if you store them in a crock under your bed.

1 cup brown sugar
1 cup butter (not margarine)
1 cup lard (not shortening)
4 cups flour

Blend sugar, butter, and lard; add flour gradually. Dough is quite stiff. Knead it as long as it takes to become smooth. Roll out on a lightly floured board — thick or thin, as you like. Cut into shapes or squares and bake at 350°F for about 10 minutes — until they are a pale gold. Don't ice, just eat.

MARY LIZ HEARN'S ALMOND SHORTBREAD

These are super; more tasty than ordinary shortbread because of the nuts — and more expensive. Try them with toasted sunflower seeds.

**3 tablespoons sugar
1 cup butter
2 cups flour
1 cup finely chopped almonds
Fine sugar for rolling**

Blend the sugar with the butter, add the flour and almonds, and work to a smooth dough with your fingers. Break off bits and roll them into small log-shaped cookies. Place them on a buttered sheet and bake at 350°F for about 20 minutes. Don't let them brown. Cool slightly and roll in fine sugar, then put them in your safest hiding place.

NORM'S CHOCOLATE CHIP MERINGUES

Whenever you have a couple of egg whites left over, you can whip up a batch of these in a few minutes. But guard them, they'll be eaten just as quickly.

**2 egg whites at room temperature
½ cup sugar
⅛ teaspoon cream of tartar
1 teaspoon vanilla
1 cup chocolate chips, more or less**

Whip up the egg whites with the sugar, cream of tartar, and vanilla until stiff but not dry. Stir in the chocolate chips and drop by spoonfuls on a foil-covered cookie sheet. Bake at 200°F for 1 hour until dry but not brown.

DATE AND NUT MERINGUES

Instead of chocolate chips, fold into the meringue ½ cup chopped dates and ½ cup chopped nuts.

FOR SPECIAL OCCASIONS

When I was an eager young housewife I used to make fancy cookies that I thought were works of art: each one was individually decorated and looked too pretty to eat, people said — though they probably didn't taste as good as they looked. Now I make the best-tasting cookies I can with the least effort and little or no decoration but a sprinkling of sugar or nuts, a nut pressed into the centre, or an icing that I can dribble over quickly.

There are times, though, like receptions, weddings, Christmas, or parties, when a plate of cookies needs more than just bulk and schmecks appeal.

FLORENTINES

I bought my first Florentine at a *pâtisserie* in Paris; I thought it the most sublime chocolate-orange confection I had ever eaten. I had another in Venice. Wherever I went on that first trip to Europe, I looked for and found more: in Lugano, Berne, Innsbruck, Munich, Heidelberg, and Cologne; I've since found some in Toronto, at the Kitchener market, and at Rundles Restaurant in Stratford. Undoubtedly they are a universal favourite. This recipe should make about thirty. Imagine having that many! I'd never before had more than one at a time. Very expensive to buy.

¾ cup of the heaviest whipping cream you can get
¼ cup sugar
¼ cup flour
½ cup blanched slivered almonds
¼ cup dessicated coconut (optional)
½ cup finely diced preserved orange peel
¼ cup sliced candied cherries (optional)
6 ounces semi-sweet chocolate

Thoroughly blend the cream and sugar; stir in the flour, almonds, coconut, and fruit. Drop dessertspoonfuls of the mixture well apart on a heavily greased and floured baking sheet. Flatten them to make them round and about 3 inches wide — they'll spread. Bake in a 350°F oven for about 10 minutes; they burn easily so keep watching and take them out when they are golden and lightly brown around the lacy edges. Leave them on the baking sheet for a few minutes to become firm but remove them before they are cold.

Melt the chocolate over hot water. Turn the cookies upside down and spread the underside with chocolate. Dry on waxed paper, bottoms up. Allow to dry overnight at room temperature if you can wait that long — I certainly couldn't.

CHINESE CHEWS

I don't know what is Chinese about these; Mother often had them when she entertained ladies.

1 cup brown sugar
2 eggs, beaten
1 cup chopped dried fruit or dates
1 cup chopped walnuts
¾ cup flour
1 teaspoon baking powder
½ teaspoon salt
Icing sugar

Add the sugar to the beaten eggs, then the fruit and nuts and the flour sifted with the baking powder and salt; mix well. Spread the dough in a buttered pan and bake in a 350°F oven for 15 minutes or until golden. Cut chews into narrow strips and roll the strips in icing sugar.

PARTY SHORTBREAD

They almost melt in your hand.

2 cups flour, less 2 tablespoonfuls
2 tablespoons cornstarch
1 cup butter
½ cup icing sugar, sifted

Combine flour with the 2 tablespoons cornstarch and sift together. Cream butter, add sugar gradually, and blend in the flour with your hands. You may need a bit more flour. Roll into cylinders and put in a cold place overnight. Cut into ⅓-inch slices and bake on a buttered pan in a 300°F oven, watching like a hawk; don't leave them too long, you don't want them to brown. When cold, ice them with a rich butter icing, flavoured with almond, and put an almond on top — or flavour icing with vanilla or rum and press a whole walnut or pecan into the icing in the centre of the cookie. Handsome.

CHOCOLATE SHORTBREAD

My own invention — and how I boasted about that when my friends asked for the recipe. Very simple — it doesn't require genius. Just add 2 squares of melted unsweetened chocolate to the butter in the PARTY SHORTBREAD recipe, then ice with chocolate butter icing made by adding melted chocolate to a left-over butter icing after you've iced the white shortbread. Put a walnut on top.

SAND COOKIES

Mother made these dainty little cookies for special occasions; over the years she must have made thousands, with infinite patience and little scalloped cookie cutters.

1 cup butter
1 scant cup light brown sugar
1 egg
1 egg yolk
2 tablespoons cold water
3½ cups flour
2 tablespoons baking powder
½ teaspoon cinnamon

Topping:
¼ cup white sugar
½ teaspoon cinnamon
1 egg white
Almonds

Blend butter and sugar; add 1 egg and 1 egg yolk, then water. Add flour sifted with baking powder and cinnamon. Roll dough thin as paper, then cut with a pretty little cutter. For topping: mix sugar with cinnamon; beat egg white slightly; blanch almonds and slice each in half. Brush each cookie with egg white, put a half-almond in the centre, and sprinkle cookie with sugar-cinnamon mixture; place on greased cookie sheets and bake in a 350°F oven till lightly browned — not very long.

SNOW DROPS

These melt in your mouth — in one bite. Some people call them Mexican Mice or Wedding Cookies.

⅞ cup butter
4 tablespoons icing sugar
2 cups cake flour
1 cup chopped nuts
2 teaspoons vanilla
1 teaspoon water

Beat butter till creamy, add sugar, then stir and blend in the flour, nuts, vanilla, and water. Chill until firm enough to shape with your fingers into small, date-shaped pieces. Bake at 350°F for 10 minutes, but watch them — remember they're *snow* drops, not coals or even golden cookies. Roll in sifted icing sugar as soon as you remove them from the oven.

ALMOND MACAROONS

Puffy and light, they'll keep for weeks if you hide them from the madding crowd.

½ cup butter
½ cup lard
½ cup white sugar
½ cup brown sugar
1 egg
2 cups flour
1 cup chopped almonds
2 teaspoons cream of tartar
1 teaspoon baking soda
¾ teaspoon almond extract
½ teaspoon salt

Cream the butter, lard, and sugars; beat in the egg and stir in the rest of the ingredients. Roll pieces about as big as acorns in your hands and put them on a greased, floured sheet. Bake in a 350°F oven for about 10 minutes or until pale gold.

CHOCOLATE MACAROONS

Tasty. Mine are sometimes tough, but always good to eat.

2 egg whites
1 cup sugar
½ teaspoon salt
½ teaspoon vanilla
1½ cups shredded coconut
1½ squares unsweetened chocolate, melted

Beat the egg whites until stiff, then fold in the sugar, salt, and vanilla and beat till mixture forms peaks. Work in the coconut and melted chocolate. Drop by teaspoonfuls on a greased, floured baking sheet and bake in a 200°F oven for about 50 minutes.

SMARTIE COOKIES

These are popular for a children's party, and I've never seen an adult turn one down.

1 cup brown sugar
½ cup white sugar
1 cup butter
2 eggs, beaten
1½ teaspoons vanilla
2½ cups flour
1 teaspoon baking soda
½ teaspoon salt
1½ cups Smarties (you could use chocolate
  or butterscotch chips)

Blend the sugars and butter, then beat in the eggs and vanilla. Sift in the flour, soda, and salt. Mix well and stir in the Smarties. Drop by teaspoonfuls on a buttered cookie sheet, put a Smartie on top of each one, and bake at 350°F for about 10 minutes.

You could let the children make these; they're not hard to do.

GUM-DROP COOKIES

Colourful, chewy, and crisp — pretty on a plate.

> ½ cup shortening
> ½ cup brown sugar
> ½ cup white sugar
> 1 egg
> 1 cup flour
> 1 teaspoon baking powder
> ½ teaspoon baking soda
> ½ teaspoon salt
> ½ cup gumdrops, cut up (no black)
> ½ cup shredded coconut
> 1 cup rolled oats
> 1 cup corn flakes

Cream shortening and sugars together. Add egg and beat until fluffy. Sift flour, baking powder, soda, and salt; add to creamed mixture and beat until well blended; then add gum-drops, coconut, rolled oats, and corn flakes. Blend into dough and drop by teaspoonfuls about 2 inches apart onto greased baking sheets. Bake at 350°F for 15 minutes. I put one bit of gum-drop on top of each cookie before baking, and when I serve them I put some of the whole gum-drops on the plate with the cookies for added colour.

EVA'S CHOCOLATE MINT COOKIES

These are neat, and her children love them — so do the grown-ups.

> ⅔ cup butter, margarine, or lard
> 1 cup white sugar
> 1 egg
> 2 cups flour
> ⅔ cup cocoa
> 1 teaspoon baking powder
> ½ teaspoon baking soda
> ½ teaspoon salt
> ¼ cup milk

Thoroughly cream the butter and sugar. Add the egg and beat well. Add the sifted dry ingredients alternately with the milk. Mix and chill. Roll to ⅛ inch thickness and cut with a fancy cutter. Bake at 350°F till crisp, about 10 minutes. Put together like a sandwich with mint filling:

½ cup icing sugar
3 or 4 teaspoons cream or milk
2 drops oil of peppermint or 1 teaspoon
  peppermint flavouring
Few grains of salt

MANDEL KUCHA (Almond Wafers)

Like crisp gold lace — with toasted-almond flavouring.

Grated rind of ½ lemon
1 cup sugar
1 cup butter
2 egg yolks
1½ cups flour

Topping:
1 egg white
1 tablespoon water
1 cup shredded almonds
½ cup sugar
2 teaspoons cinnamon
¼ teaspoon salt

Mix lemon rind with the sugar. Cream the lemon sugar with the butter and beat in the egg yolks, one at a time. Add the flour gradually, sifting it into the batter to make a rich dough. Form into little balls, half the size of a walnut, and flatten them with the bottom of a glass dipped in flour. Beat the egg white slightly with water and brush it over the cookies. Mix the almonds, the ½ cup sugar, cinnamon, and salt, and sprinkle the mixture thickly over tops of cookies. Bake in a 350°F oven until golden.

CURRANT WAFERS

Thin as net on the edges, with a thicker, curranty part in the centre.

½ cup butter
½ cup sugar
2 eggs, lightly beaten
½ teaspoon baking soda
½ cup sour cream
1 cup flour
1 cup currants
1 teaspoon vanilla

Cream butter and sugar and stir in the eggs. Stir soda into sour cream, mix with the egg-and-butter mixture, and sift in flour. Dredge currants in a very little flour and fold into batter with vanilla. Drop from a teaspoon onto a greased cookie sheet — at least 3 inches apart because they'll spread. Bake at 350°F for 10 minutes. Remove from sheet while hot. If you'd rather have cookies that are less fragile, add more flour.

THIMBLE COOKIES

One delicious bite.

½ cup butter or margarine
¼ cup sugar
1 egg white
1 cup flour
¾ cup finely chopped nuts
Tart jelly or jam

Cream the butter; add the sugar gradually and cream until light. Mix well. Work in flour. Form into small balls; dip the balls into egg white, then roll in nuts. Place on greased cookie sheet and press fairly flat with the bottom of a glass. Bake in a 300°F oven for 5 minutes. Remove from oven and make an indentation in centre of each cookie with a thimble; bake about 15 minutes longer. Cool and fill the thimble holes with a tart jelly or jam just before serving.

BESSIE'S GINGER WALNUT COOKIES

The kind you can't stop eating — crunchy, rich — nippy when you hit a piece of ginger.

⅔ cup butter
2 cups brown sugar
2 teaspoons baking soda, dissolved in
4 tablespoons boiling water
2 cups flour
2 teaspoons vanilla
½ cup chopped crystallized ginger
½ cup chopped walnuts or pecans
Red or green cherries

Mix the ingredients, except cherries, in the order given. Form into balls smaller than a walnut. Press down with a floured fork. Top each with a cherry and bake in a 325°F oven for about 15 minutes. Watch: they brown quickly.

Lorna's Treats

My friend Lorna Carruthers has given me some of her fancy recipes; she loves to make pretty, fussy little morsels to dress up a plate of goodies.

LORNA'S FILBERT FANCIES

½ pound filberts, put through the grinder
2 egg whites, unbeaten
1 cup fruit sugar
1 teaspoon vanilla

Mix all ingredients together and mould into whatever shape you think most attractive — bars, circles, crescents — keep fiddling, then bake at 350°F until golden brown.

RUM BALLS

Everyone pops one of these into their mouths on the first passing.

> 1¼ cups crushed vanilla wafers
> 1 cup icing sugar
> 1½ cups chopped pecans
> 2 tablespoons cocoa
> 2 tablespoons corn syrup
> ¼ cup rum
> ½ cup granulated sugar

Combine the finely crushed crumbs, icing sugar, pecans, and cocoa. Add the corn syrup and rum and mix well. Shape into 1-inch balls, roll in the granulated sugar, and store in a tightly covered box with a lock on it.

LORNA'S MELTING MOMENTS

These don't need chewing!

> 1 cup butter
> 1 tablespoon lard
> ½ cup icing sugar
> 2 cups sifted flour
> Pinch of baking soda
> Cherries or pecans

Cream the butter and lard. Lorna says the 1 tablespoon of lard is necessary — don't omit it. Then add the sugar gradually, beating to a cream. Add the flour with the baking soda and mix with an electric beater for fifteen minutes. Spoon onto un-buttered cookie sheets and top each one with a small piece of red or green cherry or a piece of pecan. Don't crowd them, they spread. Bake at 350°F for about 8 minutes. Handle them delicately.

MACAROON DAINTIES

Lorna says these are a Christmas special — very rich. To serve, they should be placed in those little paper bon-bon cups.

1 cup brown sugar
¼ cup butter
2 tablespoons cold water
⅛ teaspoon salt
2 cups shredded coconut
1 cup chopped candied red and green pineapple
1 cup blanched almonds
½ cup chopped mixed peel
½ cup sliced dried apricots
½ cup candied cherries
½ cup chopped dates
1 teaspoon vanilla
2 egg whites, stiffly beaten

Boil the sugar, butter, water, and salt to the soft-ball stage (235°F), approximately 5 minutes. Add the remaining ingredients, folding in the beaten egg whites at the last. Drop small teaspoonfuls on a buttered pan and bake at 275°F for about 20 minutes. Ration these or some greedy person will gobble them.

KINDERKOCHFEST

Every Oktoberfest from 1970 to 1985, the Waterloo Regional Board of Education and J.M. Schneider Inc. sponsored a Kinderkochfest Competition for Grade Seven and Eight pupils and home economics students of all the schools in Waterloo Region. Entries had to fit into one of five categories: salads and hors d'oeuvres, *Black Forest cakes and tortes, pastry and cookies, breads, and specialty German cakes. Nothing could be made with processed foods or mixes. The winners of each category, junior and senior, were given a plaque to take home and one for their school to keep for a year.*

Local dignitaries, members of the media, and members of some German Clubs were the judges. I was always invited. The sight of long tables of fancily iced cakes, tortes, and all the other delicacies — and some not so delicate — was a mouth-watering experience, until one had conscientiously tasted, as I did one year, thirty-two Black Forest cakes.

Every entry in the contest was accompanied by its recipe, which was carefully — and sometimes graphically — written by the child who had made it. I was given permission to collect prize-winning recipes — and a few others.

SCHNECKENNUDELN

These prize-winners were perfect golden spirals, little pyramids neatly glazed — a delight to behold.

2 cups milk
⅓ cup margarine or butter
1 cup sugar
1 egg, lightly beaten
1 tablespoon yeast
3 to 4 cups flour

Filling:
⅓ cup melted butter
½ cup sugar
Sprinkle of cinnamon
1 cup ground almonds

Glaze:
1 cup icing sugar
3 teaspoons water
Few drops of almond flavouring

Scald the milk. Stir in the margarine until melted. Stir in sugar and let cool to lukewarm. Blend in egg and yeast, then stir in flour a little at a time until the dough doesn't stick to the sides of the bowl. Cover and let rise in a warm place until doubled in bulk — perhaps 1 to 1½ hours. Turn the dough onto a floured surface and roll into a very thin rectangle. Brush with melted butter, then sprinkle with sugar, cinnamon, and almonds. Roll up lengthwise, as for a jelly roll. Cut into ½-inch slices and place on a buttered cookie sheet. Let rise for about 1 hour. Bake at 350°F for about 20 minutes. Watch them — they should be tinged with gold. To make glaze, combine icing sugar, water, and almond flavouring. When cookies are almost cool, brush with glaze.

VANILLEN PRETZELN (VANILLA PRETZELS)

A Grade Seven girl won a prize with these neat, sweet pretzels — a great way to keep a child busy on a rainy afternoon. This very rich cookie can also be shaped into fingers or rings and sprinkled with coloured sugar for Christmas.

5 egg yolks
1 cup + 2 tablespoons sugar
2 teaspoons vanilla
1 cup unsalted butter
4 cups sifted flour

Icing:
1 cup sifted icing sugar
1 teaspoon vanilla
1 teaspoon or more water

Beat the egg yolks with the sugar until thick and lemon-coloured. Stir in the vanilla. Cut the butter into the flour. Add the egg mixture and blend with a wooden spoon. Knead until the dough is smooth. Pinch off pieces of dough, and with floured hands roll into strips about ½ inch thick and 6 to 7 inches long. Form into pretzels and place on an ungreased cookie sheet. Bake at 350°F for about 10 to 12 minutes or until brown at the edges. Blend icing ingredients until the consistency of thick cream. Glaze pretzels while still warm.

MANDELKRANZE (ALMOND WREATHS)

Three little girls named Erika, Kim, and Petra made these neat, thin, and tempting wreaths with almonds on top.

1 cup butter
1 cup sugar
2 eggs
Grated rind of 1 lemon
2 cups flour
1 cup chopped blanched almonds

Topping:
1 egg white, unbeaten
2 tablespoons sugar
1 teaspoon cinnamon
⅓ cup chopped blanched almonds

Cream butter. Gradually beat in sugar; add eggs one at a time, beating well after each addition. Stir in grated lemon rind, flour, and 1 cup chopped almonds. Chill the dough till it is easy to roll out fairly thin on a lightly floured board. Cut with a 2½-inch doughnut cutter and place pieces on a buttered cookie sheet. Brush each wreath with unbeaten egg white and sprinkle with mixture of sugar, cinnamon, and ⅓ cup chopped almonds. Bake at 400°F for 8 minutes, or until lightly golden.

OESTERREICHISCHE LINZER PLAETZCHES (AUSTRIAN LINZER COOKIES)

These plump, mouse-coloured cookies with jam in the centre had one of the best flavours of any in the Kinderkochfest Competition.

1 cup butter
½ cup sugar
2 eggs, separated and beaten
2 cups flour
1 teaspoon cinnamon
½ teaspoon cloves
Grated rind of 1 lemon
1 cup chopped unblanched almonds, walnuts,
  or pecans
Thick raspberry jam

Cream butter. Add the sugar and beaten egg yolks. Add flour, cinnamon, cloves, and lemon rind. Form into small balls by taking a portion of dough and rolling it in the palms of your hands. Roll the ball in the beaten egg whites, then in the chopped nuts. Place on a buttered cookie sheet, and make a depression in the centre of each with a floured thimble. Fill the depression with raspberry jam. Bake at 350°F until browned — about 12 minutes — but watch them.

FOR YOUR COOKIE JAR

In a corner of my kitchen counter, I have an old black cookie jar with red cherries painted on the side. I can't say it is always full, but there are always cookies in it. As soon as I can feel the bottom layer, I get busy and make another batch just in case someone should call on me. I must have something on hand at all times: for the lawn mowers and the snow blowers; for my nieces and nephews (Kennie and Patti never fail to lift the lid of my cookie jar to see what is there); for my half-mile-away neighbour, Bonnie Bennett; for Robbie Cosford and Terrylynn Field, who live at the far end of the lake and often walk around; and for Ray Bryant with his Jehovah's Witness disciples or his wife and nine children. A full cookie jar means one is always prepared.

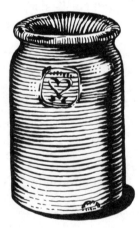

FUDGIES

These are dark and soft and chocolatey. Norm asked me for the recipe, and that is praise indeed.

¼ cup shortening
½ cup sugar, white or brown
½ cup corn syrup
1 teaspoon vanilla
1 egg
2 squares unsweetened chocolate, melted,
   or ½ cup cocoa
2 cups flour
½ teaspoon baking soda
1 teaspoon salt
½ cup buttermilk or sour milk
¾ cup chopped nuts or toasted sunflower seeds

Cream together the shortening and sugar. Add corn syrup gradually and keep beating. Blend in the vanilla, then drop in the egg and beat until light. Add the melted chocolate or cocoa. Sift together flour, soda, and salt. Add to the creamed mixture alternately with the buttermilk, beating until smooth after each addition. Stir in the nuts. Drop by teaspoonfuls onto greased baking sheets and bake at 350°F for 10 minutes. Cool on a rack or turn the cookies upside down to cool on their rounded tops.

WHOLE-WHEAT FLOUR

If you'd rather use whole-wheat flour instead of all-purpose in any or all of these recipes, that is your privilege.

ICE BOX GINGER SNAPS

Happy day when Mother made these.

½ cup each butter and lard
½ cup each brown sugar and molasses
1 teaspoon baking soda dissolved in
2 tablespoons vinegar
1 teaspoon salt
1 tablespoon powdered ginger
½ teaspoon lemon flavouring
1 teaspoon cinnamon
Sifted flour

Mix these ingredients and then add enough sifted flour to make a stiff dough. Roll into a couple of long cylinders, wrap in waxed paper, and put into fridge overnight. Slice wafer thin with a very sharp knife and bake at 400°F, watching them like a hawk, for they brown very quickly and should not be too dark.

NORM'S PEANUT BUTTER COOKIES

These are my niece Patti's favourites; Norm often bakes them for Patti to take back with her to medical school at Western.

½ cup butter
½ cup firmly packed brown sugar
½ cup white sugar
1 egg
½ cup peanut butter
1 cup roasted peanuts
1 cup flour

Cream the butter; add sugars. Beat in egg and peanut butter. Stir in peanuts. Add flour a little at a time. Mix well. Drop batter by teaspoonfuls onto lightly greased baking sheets, or roll into small balls and set on sheets. Bake at 350°F for 12 to 15 minutes, or until cookies are light brown. Watch them — they burn easily.

CHOCOLATE CRISPIES

If you want something good but haven't much time to fuss, try these.

2 squares unsweetened chocolate, melted
½ cup butter or shortening
1 cup sugar
2 eggs
½ cup sifted flour
1 teaspoon vanilla
½ teaspoon salt
½ cup chopped nuts

To melted chocolate add butter, sugar, eggs, flour, vanilla, and salt; beat well and spread on a greased baking sheet. Sprinkle nuts on top and press down a bit so they'll stick. Bake at 350°F for 15 minutes or till firm; cool slightly and cut in squares.

GLORIA LOGAN'S GRANOLA COOKIES

This recipe was sent to me in a fan letter. The cookies are healthful, with lots of fibre.

⅓ cup margarine
¼ cup honey
¼ cup brown sugar
1 egg, beaten
½ teaspoon vanilla
1 cup whole-wheat flour
¼ teaspoon baking soda
½ cup wheat germ (optional)
1 cup granola
½ to 1 cup raisins
½ cup chocolate chips (optional)

Cream margarine, honey, and sugar. Add egg and vanilla and beat well. Sift flour and soda and add to mixture. Add remaining ingredients. Drop by spoonfuls onto buttered cookie sheets and bake at 375°F for about 8 or 10 minutes.

BUTTERSCOTCH MACAROONS

Quite festive-looking — and tasty.

⅔ cup packed brown sugar
¼ cup butter
2 tablespoons water
⅓ cup chopped nuts or raisins (or both)
¼ cup chopped candied cherries
⅛ teaspoon salt
1 teaspoon vanilla
2 cups rolled oats
1 tablespoon cornstarch
2 egg whites

Cook sugar, butter, and water slowly together, stirring constantly for 5 minutes. Add nuts, cherries, salt, vanilla, rolled oats, and cornstarch. (You can substitute a cupful of coconut for a cupful of rolled oats if you like.) Mix thoroughly — the mixture will be crumbly. Beat the egg whites till stiff but not dry, and fold them into the mixture. Drop mixture by spoonfuls, an inch apart, on greased pans. Bake in a 300°F oven for about 20 minutes. Remove from pan while hot using a buttered knife.

NORM'S ORANGE COOKIES

Norm can never make these often enough to satisfy her family — and me. I think they are Norm's favourites; she always keeps some in her freezer and brings them out whenever she can't resist the urge. She says, "They're not very rich and I love them."

6 tablespoons butter
1⅓ cups sugar
Rind and juice of 2 oranges
Pinch of salt
2½ cups flour
1 teaspoon baking soda
1 cup raisins
1 cup walnuts

Mix in the order given. Drop by teaspoonfuls onto buttered cookie sheets and bake at 350°F for about 10 minutes or till they are pale gold. Watch them. Don't bake them too long. They are chewy, crisp, and wonderful.

Norm never leaves her kitchen when she's baking cookies or squares; she keeps her eye on the oven.

FIFTH ESTATE COOKIES

When a crew of five from the TV program *the fifth estate* came to film and interview me about the Cookie War, they asked me to mix up some cookie dough to put on cookie sheets for the camera. I made the easiest, whitest ones I could, and the crew enjoyed eating them as soon as they came out of the oven and had been filmed.

1 cup sugar, white or brown
¾ cup butter or margarine
¼ cup milk
1 teaspoon flavouring
1 egg
2 cups flour
1 teaspoon baking powder
½ teaspoon salt
1 cup chopped walnuts

Blend the first five ingredients, then stir in the rest till well mixed. Drop by teaspoonfuls onto ungreased cookie sheets and bake at 375°F for 8 to 12 minutes, or until slightly golden. Remove from the cookie sheet immediately.

If you like, you can use coconut as well as nuts or instead of nuts. Or use chocolate chips or finely cut gum-drops, or whatever you can think of that might be interesting.

NORM'S DATE AND NUT DROPS

These are crisp and have a good flavour. You can't stop at one or two.

1 teaspoon cinnamon
½ teaspoon baking powder
½ teaspoon cloves
½ teaspoon allspice
¼ teaspoon baking soda
¼ teaspoon salt
1 cup butter
1 cup brown sugar
2 eggs
2 cups chopped nuts
2 cups chopped dates
2 tablespoons orange or lemon juice
1½ cups flour (half could be whole wheat)

Blend butter, sugar, and eggs, and beat well. Add nuts and dates, stir in the juice, then the dry ingredients, sifted together. Drop by teaspoonfuls well apart on a buttered baking sheet. (They spread.) Bake in a 375°F oven for 12 to 15 minutes.

TEMPTERS

Crisp coconut cookies with chocolate chips — and nuts, if you like.

½ cup shortening
1 cup sugar
1 egg, beaten
1 teaspoon vanilla
¼ teaspoon almond extract
2 tablespoons milk
2 cups pastry flour or 1¾ cups all-purpose flour
1½ teaspoons baking powder
½ teaspoon salt
1 cup shredded coconut
½ cup chocolate chips
½ cup chopped nuts (optional)

Cream shortening until light and fluffy, then blend in sugar; beat in egg, vanilla, almond extract, and milk. Sift the dry ingredients and add, a third at a time, combining well after each addition. Mix in the coconut, chocolate chips, and nuts. Drop teaspoonfuls of dough onto greased cookie sheets and press flat with a wet fork. Bake in 350°F oven until golden — about 12 minutes.

FRUIT JUMBLES

Mother loved these soft, spicy drop cookies; she made them more often than any other — and in big batches. Norm makes them, too.

¾ **cup butter**
1½ **cups brown sugar**
2 **or 3 eggs**
1 **teaspoon vanilla**
2 **tablespoons milk**
Pinch of salt
2 **cups chopped dates**
1 **cup chopped walnuts**
3 **cups flour**
1 **teaspoon baking soda**
1 **teaspoon cinnamon**
½ **teaspoon cloves**
½ **teaspoon nutmeg**

Mother's recipe gives no directions for mixing except to sift the soda and spices with the flour after mixing the rest in the order given. Drop spoonfuls onto buttered cookie sheets and bake at 350°F for about 12 minutes; don't overbake or they'll be too dry.

TOASTED BEECHNUT COOKIES

But who has beechnuts these days? We used to spread blankets under the trees in the bush, and Daddy would shake down the nuts. Mother patiently opened them with a sharp knife and toasted them in the oven. If you haven't a beech tree handy, you could use toasted almonds.

¼ **cup shortening**
½ **cup sugar**
2 **egg yolks (or 1 whole egg), beaten**
1 **teaspoon lemon juice (optional)**
1 **cup flour**
1½ **teaspoons baking powder**
½ **teaspoon salt**
¼ **cup milk**
2 **cups toasted nuts**

Cream the shortening, add sugar and beaten yolks, and then add the lemon juice. Sift the flour with the baking powder and salt; add, with milk, to the mixture. Add toasted nuts. Drop by spoonfuls onto a greased cookie sheet. Bake at 350°F for 10 minutes.

ORANGE DROP COOKIES

It's nice to have these to vary your flavours when you serve a plateful of cookies.

¾ **cup shortening**
¼ **cup butter**
1½ **cups brown sugar**
2 **eggs, beaten**
¼ **cup orange juice**
Grated rind of 1 orange
1 **teaspoon vanilla**
1 **cup buttermilk or sour milk**
3½ **cups flour**
1 **teaspoon baking soda**
¼ **teaspoon baking powder**
1 **cup chopped dates**
1 **cup chopped nuts**

Cream shortening, butter, and sugar; add eggs, orange juice, rind, vanilla, and milk. Add sifted dry ingredients, then dates and nuts. Drop from a teaspoon onto a greased cookie sheet. Bake in a 350°F oven for 15 minutes. To make them look pretty, you might put a paper-thin cross of orange rind on each cookie or half a walnut.

OLD MENNONITE FAVOURITES

Bevvy bakes batches of cookies every week. She puts them on her table three times a day, and whenever Lyddie and Amsey have a hungry feeling between meals, they reach into her cookie boxes and help themselves to a plump ginger cookie or a handful of pfeffernusse. Almost half of Bevvy's little hand-written cookbook is made up of cookie recipes: most of them use rolled oats, molasses, spices, or raisins; the rest are plain sugar cookies, kisses, or squares.

JAM JAMS

These are chewy and have a tantalizing, old-fashioned flavour.
I think it's the lard that does it.

1 cup lard
1 cup brown sugar
⅓ cup molasses
1 teaspoon lemon or vanilla extract
2 eggs
4 cups flour
2 teaspoons baking soda
Apple butter or jam

Blend lard and sugar, then molasses, lemon, and eggs. Add flour
sifted with soda. The dough should be easy to handle. Roll it out
until quite thin and cut into rounds. Bake on a greased sheet at
325°F for 7 minutes, then look — it might take a minute more
for the cookies to turn crisp and brown. While they are still
warm, put two together with apple butter or jam spread between them. They become soft and keep well.

NANCY MARTIN'S POTATO CHIP COOKIES

Nancy is a friend of Eva and Hannah's. She loves to read books
and to try new recipes on her father, Mathias, who has a great
collection of bells and bottles in his leather-working shop near
Hawkesville.

2 cups softened margarine
1 cup sugar
3¼ cups flour
3 teaspoons vanilla
1 cup crushed potato chips

Cream the margarine and sugar till real fluffy. Mix in all the rest
and drop by teaspoonfuls onto an ungreased cookie sheet. Press
lightly with a fork dipped in cold water. Bake at 350°F for 8 to
10 minutes. Remove from oven and leave on sheet a few minutes
to cool. Nancy said, "This is supposed to make 90 cookies."

EVA'S CHEWY MOLASSES COOKIES

"We just love these," Eva told me. "They're best made with apple molasses."

1 cup molasses
1 cup brown sugar
2 eggs, beaten
2 teaspoons baking soda
Flour to make a soft dough
White sugar

Mix the first five ingredients in the order given. Roll dough into balls and dip in white sugar. Bake on buttered cookie sheets at 350°F for about 10 or 12 minutes. When cold, put the cookies into a crock. Cover it with a cloth till the cookies are soft and chewy, then cover tightly.

DANIEL'S GINGER CRINKLES

Hard, with cracks in their sugar coating, and very tasty.

¾ cup lard
1 cup brown sugar
1 egg
¼ cup molasses
2¼ cups flour
2 teaspoons baking soda
½ teaspoon salt
1 teaspoon cinnamon
1 teaspoon ginger
½ teaspoon cloves
White sugar

Blend lard and sugar; add egg and molasses and beat until blended. Sift flour, soda, salt, and spices; add to creamed mixture and blend thoroughly. Put the dough in a cold place till it is well chilled. Shape into balls the size of hickory nuts, roll them in white sugar and put 2 inches apart on a greased baking sheet, pressing them a bit flat with a fork. Bake at 350°F for 12 to 15 minutes. Wonderful with apple sauce.

SHORT CAKES

I copied this straight from Bevvy's book.

1 quart flour
A good handful of lard (How do you like that?)
1½ cups sugar
1 teaspoon baking soda
Buttermilk to roll out
1 cup currants
2 teaspoons baking powder

There were no directions — Bevvy doesn't need them. I blended 1 cup of lard with the flour, soda, baking powder, and sugar. I stirred in the currants — adding an extra ½ cup — then enough buttermilk to make a dough I could roll thin with a rolling pin. I cut them into rounds with a tin, placed them on a greased cookie sheet, and baked them at 350°F for about 10 minutes, keeping my eye on them. They were really good — like pastry wafers.

CHEWY MOLASSES COOKIES

Bevvy makes these big and round.

¾ cup shortening
1 cup sugar
2 eggs, beaten
1 cup molasses
4 cups flour
2 teaspoons cinnamon
1 teaspoon salt
1 teaspoon baking soda
1 teaspoon ginger
¾ cup cold, strong coffee
Walnuts

Cream shortening and sugar, add eggs and molasses; beat well. Add sifted dry ingredients alternately with coffee. Drop from a teaspoon onto a greased cookie sheet. Put a walnut on top of each for a prize and bake in a 350°F oven for 15 minutes.

RIGGLEVAKE KUCHA (Railroad Cookies)

This is the now-famous Old Mennonite cookie recipe that involved Eva, Hannah, and many other Mennonite ladies and me in the Great Cookie War between Procter & Gamble and Nabisco. There was much press, TV, and radio coverage; the story I wrote about it for *Saturday Night* magazine won a National Magazine Award and was reprinted in my book *Schmecks Appeal*. A play based on the story was produced at Ontario's Blyth Festival and a feature-length movie is waiting for funding.

I have never made Rigglevake Kucha; they are rather fussy and make a large batch. When Mennonites made them for the lawyers, they had cookies all over their kitchens. When I was in Comox, British Columbia, in October, the Blue Heron bookstore advertised a Rigglevake cookie baking contest and the contestants said the recipe gave them enough cookies to last until Christmas, though the rolls of dough could have been frozen and kept until the festive season.

The cookie is a neat little pinwheel. Eva and Hannah put the light part on the bottom because when baked it is crisp and doesn't break away from the edge of the cookie as the soft dark part would do. To keep their cookies round, they cut the cookies with a thread!

Light part:
1 cup butter
1 cup white sugar
1 egg
½ cup milk
½ teaspoon vanilla
2 teaspoons baking powder

Dark part:
1 cup butter
1 cup brown sugar
1 cup molasses
½ cup water
½ teaspoon vanilla
2 teaspoons baking soda

Enough flour in each part to make dough easy to handle.

Mix the light and dark parts in separate bowls. Blend the butter and sugar for both parts. For the light part, beat in the egg, then alternately add the milk, vanilla, and baking powder sifted with flour. For the dark part, add to the butter-sugar mixture the molasses, water, and vanilla alternately with baking soda sifted with flour.

Break off pieces of dough from both dark and light parts, shape them into rounds, and roll them separately about ⅛ inch thick. Put one on top of the other, roll up like a jelly roll, and slice off pieces as thinly as you can. Place on greased cookie sheets and bake at 350°F till done.

SELINA'S CINNAMON CRINKLES

When Selina wants to be fancy, she rolls the dough into balls. When she wants to be smart, she rolls the dough into a cylinder and slices it. Either way, these taste good.

½ cup lard
1¼ cups brown sugar
¼ cup apple molasses or store-bought molasses
1 egg
1½ tablespoons sour cream
1 teaspoon vanilla
2½ cups flour
1 teaspoon baking soda
1 teaspoon cinnamon
Sugar
Peel or nuts (optional)

Cream the lard and sugar. Beat in the molasses, egg, sour cream, and vanilla. Stir in the flour, sifted with the soda and cinnamon. (All very easy if you have a food processor.) Chill the dough thoroughly, then roll it into a cylinder and slice it, or make little balls the size of hickory nuts. Roll slices or balls in sugar. Place 2 inches apart on a buttered cookie sheet. Trim with a bit of peel or nut, if you like. Bake at 350°F for 10 minutes.

SALOME'S MONSTER COOKIES

Salome enclosed this recipe with her Christmas card. She wrote:
"Knowing you like to eat and try recipes that are different, here
is one that is flying through our Old Order Mennonite community at a great rate. People make half batches and still have
cookies all over the place. Mix them in a very large dishpan and
you'll have anywhere from 300 to 600 cookies, depending on the
size. Best of all they taste delicious."

> **2 cups margarine**
> **4½ cups brown sugar**
> **4 cups white sugar**
> **1 dozen eggs**
> **3 pounds peanut butter**
> **2½ tablespoons baking soda**
> **18 cups rolled oats**
> **1 pound chocolate chips**
> **½ cup vanilla**
> **2 cups peanuts or other nuts**
> **1 pound Smarties**

Combine the margarine, sugars, eggs, and peanut butter, then
add the remaining ingredients except the Smarties, which are
more colourful if put on top of each cookie. Drop by teaspoons
onto buttered cookie sheets, top each with a Smartie, and bake
at 350°F for 10 minutes.

Salome wrote, "Vera, my son's wife, and I made half a batch
together and still have lots. You should try them sometime
when you want a lot of cookies."

ROLLED OATS COOKIES

You can't beat a good oatmeal cookie: flavourful, rich, and not too sweet, they have a fine texture, and keep well. After going through my cookie recipes, I found that more than thirty require rolled oats. A number have similar ingredients and are prepared in the same way. You might pick your own favourites or make your own variations or substitutions from these:

OATMEAL DROP COOKIES

	CRISP	CHEWY
Shortening	¾ cup	½ cup lard
Brown sugar	1½ cups	1 cup
Buttermilk (or water)	6 tablespoons	¼ cup water
Salt	1 teaspoon	½ teaspoon
Rolled oats	3 cups	2 cups
Raisins		1 cup
Flour	1½ cups	1 cup
Baking soda	¾ teaspoon	1 teaspoon

	MY FAVOURITE	BEVVY'S BEST
Shortening	1 cup	1 cup bacon fat
Brown sugar	2 cups	1 cup
Eggs	2, beaten	
Vanilla or rum	1 teaspoon	1 teaspoon
Buttermilk (or water)	5 teaspoons	2 tablespoons warm water
Salt	1 teaspoon	Pinch
Rolled oats	3 cups	3 cups
Raisins	1 cup	
Walnuts	1 cup	
Cinnamon	1 teaspoon	
Flour	2 cups	1½ cups
Baking soda	1 teaspoon	1 teaspoon

Blend the shortening and sugar; add eggs, vanilla, buttermilk or water, and salt; mix in the rolled oats, raisins, walnuts, and cinnamon; then the flour and soda, sifted together. Drop by teaspoonfuls onto greased cookie sheets, flattening each cookie with a fork (you don't want them thick). Bake at 350°F until lightly browned — 8 to 10 minutes. Don't pile them in layers in your cookie jar until they are completely cold or they'll lose their crispness.

OATMEAL CARAMEL COOKIES

Quick and easy: the first recipe I pasted in my book when I was married. Delicious.

½ cup melted butter
1 cup brown sugar
1 teaspoon vanilla
2 cups rolled oats
½ teaspoon baking powder

Mix all together and press into a greased, floured cookie sheet with sides (the dough is really just crumbs at this stage). Bake in a 400°F oven and the batter will melt together till it's golden and the smell is divine — just a few minutes (watch carefully). As soon as you take it from the oven, cut in squares and remove them from the pan while they're hot. They'll be crisp and scrummy. Their thickness depends on the size of your pan — they're good ½ an inch thick, better with more of them if they are thinner.

BARBIE'S SUPER SIMPLE OATMEAL COOKIES

These are Barbie's stand-bys. She — or Patti or Kennie — whips them up in no time to keep the cookie jar full. Which means they make them very often.

1 cup margarine (or half butter)
½ cup brown sugar
½ cup white sugar or brown
1 egg
1 teaspoon salt
1 teaspoon baking soda
1 cup flour
2½ cups rolled oats (or 1 cup coconut and
    1½ cups rolled oats)
1 teaspoon vanilla

Mix everything together, roll pieces in balls and press down with a fork on a buttered cookie sheet. Bake at 350°F till golden, about 12 minutes. Barbie always doubles the recipe or she'd be making more the next day.

RAISIN OATMEAL MOLASSES COOKIES

These have lots of flavour, are very crisp, and stay that way.

½ cup margarine or butter
1¼ cups sugar
2 eggs
⅓ cup molasses
1 teaspoon vanilla
½ teaspoon salt
2 cups rolled oats
1¾ cups flour
1 teaspoon baking powder
1 teaspoon baking soda
½ cup raisins
½ cup chopped walnuts

Blend margarine and sugar well. Beat in eggs, molasses, vanilla, and salt. Stir in the oats, then the flour, sifted with the baking powder and soda. Stir in raisins and walnuts. Drop by spoonfuls — far apart — onto a greased and floured cookie sheet. Then bake at 325°F for 12 to 15 minutes — but watch them. These are good keepers — if you hide them.

SCOTTIES

These are hard at first, but good eating for a long time.

1¾ cups flour
¼ teaspoon salt
2 teaspoons baking powder
½ teaspoon cinnamon
¼ teaspoon nutmeg
¼ teaspoon cloves
1¾ cups rolled oats
1 cup sliced dates
½ cup chopped nuts
½ cup shortening
1 cup sugar
1 egg, beaten
2 tablespoons milk

Sift together the flour, salt, baking powder, and spices; add the oats, dates, and nuts; mix well. Cream the shortening, add the sugar gradually, then the egg. Work the dry ingredients into the creamed mixture with the milk (you may need a bit more milk). Drop by teaspoonfuls two inches apart onto a well-greased baking sheet and bake in a 400°F oven for almost 10 minutes.

KITCHEN SINK COOKIES

"So called because you can add whatever you like and they always seem to be a success," Nancy writes about her recipe. "These are my favourite cookies, and I've tried a lot. They are for people who love chocolate but want a combination of healthy ingredients; they keep long because of the honey. I think they are dynamite!"

1 cup whole wheat flour
¼ cup soy flour
1⅓ cups rolled oats
¼ cup milk powder
½ teaspoon salt
1½ teaspoons cinnamon
½ teaspoon ground nutmeg and cloves
⅔ cup raisins
⅔ cup chocolate chips
2 eggs
¼ cup oil or melted butter
¼ cup honey
¼ cup molasses

Options to be added (just about anything):
Nancy prefers ¼ cup peanuts
or ⅓ cup sunflower seeds
or ¾ cup coconut
or ¼ cup sesame seeds

Mix all the dry ingredients, including your choice of options. Beat the eggs; add oil, honey, molasses, and beat. Pour liquid into dry ingredients and stir till moistened. If mixture is too dry, add milk or water. Drop onto ungreased cookie sheets. Bake in a 350°F oven for 10 to 12 minutes.

NUTTY ROLLED-OAT COOKIES

These are very simple. Everyone who tastes them says they taste like nuts, although there are no nuts in them.

>1 tablespoon butter
>1 cup sugar
>2 eggs, separated
>2½ cups rolled oats
>2 teaspoons baking powder
>1 teaspoon vanilla

Cream the butter and sugar; add the egg yolks, oats, baking powder, and vanilla. Beat the egg whites until stiff and add last. Drop by teaspoonfuls — far apart — onto buttered and floured cookie sheets. Bake at 300°F for 10 minutes or until golden brown. (If you're lazy — as I am — you might simply beat the eggs and mix with the other ingredients.)

SUNFLOWER SEED COOKIES

I seem to persist in calling these Birdseed Cookies — I suppose because before dawn every morning in winter I put on my boots, coat, kerchief, and gloves and go out on my patio to fill up three bird feeders with sunflower seeds for the cardinals, jays, grosbeaks, chickadees, juncos, finches, nuthatches, and unwelcome squirrels that will soon come for their breakfasts — which last all day. Every winter I put out 400 pounds of seed.

 These cookies are surprisingly good — for people.

>½ cup butter or margarine
>1 cup brown sugar
>1 egg
>1 tablespoon milk
>1 teaspoon vanilla
>1 cup flour
>½ teaspoon baking soda
>½ teaspoon baking powder
>½ teaspoon salt
>1 cup rolled oats
>1 cup toasted sunflower seeds — shelled, of course

Cream the butter and sugar. Beat in the egg, milk, and vanilla; add the sifted dry ingredients, and then the oats and sunflower seeds to the creamed mixture. Mix all together. Drop by teaspoonfuls onto buttered cookie sheets. Bake at 350°F for 7 to 10 minutes. They should be lightly gold on top and slightly puffed up. They stay crisp if you put them into a tightly closed tin.

CAROL HUDGINS'S OWN COOKIES

When I came home from town one summer evening, I found a little plastic packet of cookies fastened to my door knocker. Who was the cookie fairy? After tasting the cookies I wanted the recipe. Next day Carol came down the lake in her sailboat and wrote it for me. She is a home economist; the cookies are her own invention.

¾ cup butter
1 cup brown sugar
1 large egg
1 teaspoon vanilla
1 cup rolled oats
¼ cup soy flour or ¼ cup wheat germ
¼ cup milk powder
¾ cup whole wheat flour
2 teaspoons baking powder
1 teaspoon salt
1½ cups of any mixture of chocolate chips,
**   sesame seeds, sunflower seeds, raisins,**
**   dates, walnuts, peanuts, or any chopped nuts**

Cream the butter and sugar, then beat in the egg and vanilla. Combine the rolled oats, soy flour or wheat germ, milk powder, whole wheat flour, baking powder, and salt. Stir into the creamed mixture and add as much as you like — about 1½ cups altogether — of any mixture of the chocolate chips, seeds, fruit, or nuts. Either drop by teaspoonfuls onto a buttered cookie sheet or roll into a cylinder, wrap in waxed paper, put in fridge, and slice and bake as needed. Bake at 350°F for about 12 minutes.

BUTTER MEAL COOKIES

This is one of my stand-bys; I make them whenever I have chicken fat on hand — no other shortening gives them quite the delicacy.

> ½ cup chicken fat or butter
> 1 cup brown sugar
> 2 teaspoons vanilla (almost)
> ¼ cup boiling water, to which you have added
> 1 scant teaspoon baking soda
> 2 cups flour
> 2 cups rolled oats
> Pinch of salt

Blend the fat with the sugar; add the vanilla and boiling water and soda. Add the flour, oats, and salt, and mix well. Drop by spoonfuls onto a greased cookie sheet and pat out as thin as possible, using your hand or a fork dipped in flour. Bake in a 350°F oven till golden brown — just a few minutes.

PATTI'S SPREADIES

Patti loves these. They spread *big*. If taste means more than shape, these are tremendous.

> ⅔ cup raisins
> ¾ cup butter or margarine
> 1 cup sugar
> 1 egg, beaten
> ½ teaspoon lemon juice or vanilla
> ¼ cup molasses
> 2 tablespoons tea or water
> 1½ cups flour
> 1 teaspoon baking soda
> ¼ teaspoon salt
> 1 teaspoon ginger
> 1 teaspoon cinnamon
> 1 cup rolled oats
> ½ cup chocolate chips

Soak raisins in hot water until soft. Drain and set aside. Cream butter and sugar. Add egg, lemon juice, molasses, and tea; blend well. Sift together the dry ingredients and stir into the creamed mixture. Add the oats, chocolate chips, and raisins, and mix well. Drop by teaspoonfuls onto buttered cookie sheets. Dip a fork in hot water and press the cookies flat, though they may spread out by themselves. Bake at 325°F for about 8 to 10 minutes. Don't overbake. Try to leave a few to cool off.

KRISPIE CRACKLES

This recipe makes a big boxful of cookies, and every time Patti and Ken come to my house they open the box, take two or three cookies, and say, "Gee, these cookies are good." The first time I made them, the cookies ran together on the cookie sheets. I scraped them off the pans as quickly as I could while they were very hot and broke them in pieces. The resulting cookies were ragged-looking but delicious. So, who cares?

1 cup butter or margarine
1 cup brown sugar
1 cup white sugar
2 eggs
2 teaspoons vanilla
1½ cups flour
1 teaspoon baking powder
1 teaspoon baking soda
2 cups rolled oats
1 cup coconut
2 cups Rice Krispies

Cream butter and sugars. Beat in eggs and vanilla. Sift together and add flour, baking powder, and soda. Stir in oats, coconut, and Rice Krispies. Drop by teaspoonfuls — far apart — onto a buttered and floured cookie sheet. Bake at 350°F for almost 10 minutes, or until golden brown.

MUNCHIE CRUNCHIE COOKIES

These have plenty of fibre and flavour. Kids love them — and so do I.

> **1 cup margarine or butter**
> **¾ cup sugar**
> **2 eggs**
> **1 teaspoon vanilla**
> **2 cups flour**
> **½ teaspoon baking powder**
> **1 teaspoon baking soda**
> **½ teaspoon salt**
> **¼ cup wheat germ**
> **2 cups rolled oats**
> **3 cups Special K cereal or bran**
> **1 cup shredded coconut**
> **1 cup chopped nuts**

Beat margarine and sugar till creamy. Add eggs and vanilla and stir well. Add remaining ingredients. Mix till well blended. Drop by teaspoonfuls onto an ungreased cookie sheet. Bake at 350°F for 8 to 10 minutes.

MAGGIE'S ROLL AND SLICE COOKIES

In Neil's Harbour, Maggie's son copied this recipe for me; he told me, "There ain't none made better than these." Maggie said, "Keith, don't say ain't."

> **¾ cup lard**
> **1 cup firmly packed brown sugar**
> **½ cup white sugar**
> **2 eggs**
> **1 teaspoon vanilla**
> **1½ cups flour**
> **1 teaspoon baking soda**
> **1 teaspoon salt**
> **3 cups oatmeal or rolled oats**
> **1 cup chopped raisins or dates (optional)**
> **1 cup chocolate or butterscotch chips (optional)**

Cream the lard and sugars together until light; add the eggs and vanilla, beating well. Stir in the flour, soda, and salt sifted together, stirring until the mixture is smooth. Mix in the oatmeal and any or all of the other ingredients. Form into a roll, chill for a while, then slice as thin as you can. Arrange on buttered cookie sheets — they spread — and bake in a 350°F oven for 8 to 10 minutes. You should have 109: Keith says, "And that ain't never enough."

NORM'S NUTRITIOUS COOKIES

These are the best nutritious cookies I've ever eaten. They have a crumbly top and stay crisp. Norm has to freeze them to keep them longer than a day. We just can't stop eating them.

½ cup butter
½ cup shortening
1 cup white sugar
1 cup brown sugar
2 cups rolled oats
¾ cup desiccated coconut
2 eggs
1 teaspoon baking powder
1 teaspoon baking soda
½ teaspoon salt
1 teaspoon vanilla
½ to 1 cup mixed peel or raisins or chopped prunes
    or chopped nuts — or a combination
½ cup wheat germ
1½ cups flour, stirred but unsifted

Cream the butter and shortening with the sugars. Then add all the other ingredients in the order given, beating all the time (at low speed with an electric mixer if you have one). Butter cookie sheets and drop batter by heaping teaspoonfuls at least 1½ inches apart. Don't crowd them. Bake at 350°F for 10 minutes — but watch them.

ALEDA WEBER'S TASTY OAT COOKIES

These have a very good flavour but are a little hard to bite at
first. Great with apple sauce.

1 cup vegetable oil
1½ cups honey or brown sugar
2 teaspoons vanilla
½ teaspoon salt
2½ cups flour
1½ teaspoons cinnamon
½ cup milk
4 cups rolled oats
½ cup chopped walnuts
¼ cup sunflower seeds

Cream together oil, honey, vanilla, and salt. Add flour, cinnamon, and milk, stirring until well mixed. When smooth, add
rolled oats, nuts, and seeds. Drop by spoonfuls onto buttered
cookie sheets and bake at 350°F for 10 minutes, or until golden.

ROLLED OATMEAL COOKIES WITH FILLING

	TRILBY'S	LOVINA'S
	With filling baked in	
Shortening	1 cup	1 cup
Sugar	1 cup white	1½ cups brown
Flour	2½ cups	2 cups
Baking soda or powder	1 teaspoon baking soda	1 teaspoon baking soda
Salt	½ teaspoon	½ teaspoon
Rolled oats	2½ cups	3 cups
Milk or water	1 cup sweet milk	½ cup water

	MOTHER'S	**BEVVY'S**
	Filled after baking	
Shortening	1 cup	1 cup
Sugar	1 cup brown	1 cup brown
Flour	2 cups	3 cups (almost)
Baking soda or powder	1 teaspoon baking soda	3 teaspoons baking powder
Salt	½ teaspoon	½ teaspoon
Rolled oats	2 cups	2 cups
Milk or water	¼ cup sour milk	½ cup sweet milk

Cream shortening and sugar together. Sift dry ingredients together and stir them into the creamed mixture along with the rolled oats and milk or water. Chill if the dough is too sticky to roll. Roll out to ⅛ of an inch thickness. For Trilby's and Lovina's cookies, use a cutter about three inches in diameter; put a teaspoon of the date filling (recipe below) on one side, fold the other side over, and pinch the filling into the cookie; place on a greased cookie sheet and bake at 350°F till golden brown. For Mother's and Bevvy's, use a small cutter and bake on greased cookie sheets at 350°F for about 10 minutes. When baked and cooled, put them together in pairs with date filling between — but wait until you are ready to serve them, or they'll become limp.

DATE FILLING

2 cups cut-up dates
½ cup sugar, brown or white
½ cup water
2 tablespoons lemon or orange juice (optional)
1 teaspoon vanilla

Cook together slowly, stirring until thick — about 5 minutes. This keeps well in the fridge.

FILLED OATMEAL CRISPS

Not fancy, but a bit fussy. They always get raves.

**2½ cups rolled oats finely ground through
    food chopper or processor
1 teaspoon baking soda
1 teaspoon baking powder
¼ teaspoon salt
½ cup shortening
1½ cups light brown sugar
½ cup sour cream**

Mix oats with soda, baking powder, and salt. Cream shortening
with sugar and blend in oats mixture. Add sour cream and work
into a stiff dough. Chill for at least 2 hours. Roll very thin on a
lightly floured board, cut, and lift *carefully* onto greased baking
sheets — the dough is very tender. Bake in a 400°F oven for 8
minutes — watch it! Remove from pans. When cold, put two
cookies together with a thin layer of the following delicious
filling:

**½ pound dates
½ pound figs
1 cup brown sugar
2 tablespoons boiling water
2 tablespoons lemon juice
½ cup finely ground walnuts
1 tablespoon butter
1 teaspoon grated orange rind**

Cut dates and figs into small pieces, mix in saucepan with sugar,
water, lemon juice, and nuts. Cook gently, about 15 minutes,
until thick and clear, stirring often. Add butter and orange rind,
then cool. I don't spread this on the cookies until I'm ready to
serve them or they'll become soft. I like them crisp, with that
soft, tasty filling squishing between them. These are really
terrific.

UNBAKED COOKIES AND SQUARES

These are a lifesaver if you need something to serve in a hurry. I usually make them in summer when it's hot and I don't want to turn on my oven and heat my house. Besides all those reasons, they are very, very good.

RUBY'S PEANUT KRISPIE SQUARES

At Christmas, Ruby brought me a pretty plastic dish full of cookies — seven different kinds. These were my favourites.

½ cup peanut butter
½ cup corn syrup
½ cup brown sugar
⅓ cup butter
2 cups Rice Krispies
1 cup nuts (Ruby used pecans, but peanuts will do)
Chocolate icing (optional)

Over low heat, combine peanut butter, corn syrup, sugar, and butter, stirring until mixture is hot and the sugar is melted. Pour over the Rice Krispies and nuts and stir until evenly coated. Press into a buttered 8" x 8" pan. Let cool. Frost them with chocolate icing if you want to be fancy, but they don't need it. Cut in squares and eat half a dozen at a time.

I always keep a large box of Rice Krispies in my cupboard because I love Rice Krispie squares. They are so easy and quick to make because they need no baking.

CHOCOLATE MARSHMALLOW SQUARES

Norm says that these are rich and good like candy, and don't need baking.

2 cups chocolate chips
1 cup icing sugar
½ cup butter
1 egg, beaten
2 cups miniature marshmallows
Graham wafers
Chopped walnuts

Melt chocolate chips, icing sugar, and butter. Cool. Add egg and marshmallows. Place graham wafers in the bottom of a 9" x 9" pan. Spread mixture on top. Sprinkle top with chopped walnuts. Chill. Cut in squares.

CHOCOLATE KRISPIE CRACKLES

You can make these in 5 minutes, and rationalize as you eat half a dozen that they are just breakfast cereal. I've often eaten a whole panful myself in two days. I just keep nibbling away.

¼ cup cocoa
3 tablespoons butter
¼ cup corn syrup
¼ cup white or brown sugar
3 cups Rice Krispies
½ cup nuts (optional)

Combine the cocoa, butter, corn syrup, and sugar in a saucepan; cook over low heat, stirring until the mixture comes to a boil. No longer. Remove from the heat, add the cereal and nuts, and stir until they are coated. Pour into a buttered 9" x 9" pan, pat down, and cut into squares. Or drop spoonfuls on waxed paper till they're set. The latter is risky, someone might snitch.

PEANUT BUTTER KRISPIE COOKIES

Norm has so many quick-to-make cookie recipes — these are as quickly eaten!

1 cup brown sugar
½ cup corn syrup
½ cup peanut butter
1 teaspoon vanilla
2 cups Rice Krispies
½ cup chopped walnuts
Chocolate butter icing

Dissolve the sugar, syrup, and peanut butter on the stove slowly; then add the vanilla, cereal, and walnuts. Mix quickly and pat into a greased, square cake pan. Don't bake. Ice with chocolate butter icing and cut into squares — if they last that long.

CHOCOLATE GRAHAM WAFER BALLS

Small balls are fiddly things to make, but in this case they're worth it. You don't have to bake them — just make them and eat them.

½ cup corn syrup
¼ cup butter
2 cups chocolate chips, semi-sweet or regular
¼ teaspoon salt
1 teaspoon vanilla
3 cups graham wafer crumbs
1 cup chopped raisins
½ cup chopped walnuts or pecans

In a double boiler over hot water, blend the syrup, butter, and chocolate chips, stirring occasionally until the chocolate is melted. Remove from heat and add salt and vanilla. Cool slightly before adding crumbs, raisins, and nuts. Mix well, then shape into small balls and place on a cookie sheet and chill thoroughly.

You don't have to keep them cold indefinitely. They won't last long enough.

FUNERAL COOKIES

Not a bit funereal but the quickest thing to make and take to a suddenly bereaved friend who might need to have "something on hand."

3 cups rolled oats
1 cup coconut
½ cup walnuts
½ cup raisins (optional)
2 cups sugar
½ cup shortening
½ cup cocoa
½ cup milk
½ teaspoon salt
1 teaspoon vanilla

Mix rolled oats, coconut, walnuts, and raisins. Bring the sugar, shortening, cocoa, milk, and salt to a rolling boil — no more than that. Remove the saucepan from the heat, add the vanilla, and then the mixed dry ingredients. Stir together quickly to a crumbly mass and drop by spoonfuls onto your kitchen counter or waxed paper, working quickly before it cools and hardens. The dropped cookies may be a bit ragged: let them be; there isn't time to repair them till you've dropped all of the mixture. Press each cookie together with your fingers while it's still warm to give it a more regular shape and to be sure it hangs together.

If you want a change, you can use only a third of a cup of shortening in the boiled part, and when you take it off the heat stir in, until melted, a third of a cup of peanut butter, and use peanuts instead of walnuts.

FRUIT AND NUT BALLS

When Bob and Carol Hudgins called on me recently, they told me about the wonderful cookies Bob makes in their food processor. So easy and so good for you. Bob is a chemistry professor, and Carol is a nutritionist.

Bob puts **nuts** into the processor bowl, any kind of nuts and any reasonable amount — almonds, walnuts, sunflower seeds, Brazils, whatever he happens to have. Then he adds **fruit** — raisins, dates, dried apricots, prunes, whatever. He turns on the machine, and lets it go until all is well blended and malleable. If there are too many nuts, he adds more fruit — and vice versa. When the mixture sticks together, he forms it into small balls with his fingers. And that's it. Delicious. And what could be purer?

CHEESE SNACKS

There's only one problem with cheese cookies: you can't stop eating them until the whole batch is gone.

CHEESE NETTIES

When Kit and Vern come from Brantford for afternoon tea, Kit often brings these. We gobble them up with our drinks.

> **1 cup shredded sharp Cheddar cheese**
> **½ cup softened butter**
> **⅛ teaspoon Worcestershire sauce**
> **Salt to taste (sometimes the cheese is salty enough)**
> **¾ cup flour**
> **2 cups Rice Krispies**

Mix the cheese, butter, Worcestershire sauce, and salt. Stir in the flour and cereal. Mix well, then roll the dough into a log 1½ inches in diameter. Wrap the log in waxed paper and put it in the fridge for at least 30 minutes. Cut the log in ¼-inch slices and place them on a lightly buttered baking sheet. Bake at 350°F for 10 minutes or until lightly browned.

You can double this recipe if you like but be prepared to spoil your appetite for dinner or whatever else you had planned to eat with afternoon tea.

NIPPY CHEESE BITS

These are tangy and light.

> **½ cup butter or margarine**
> **¾ cup all-purpose or whole wheat flour**
> **1 cup finely grated nippy cheese**
> **Pinch of cayenne pepper**
> **¼ teaspoon salt**
> **2 cups Rice Krispies**
> **Nuts or cheese**

Blend the butter with the flour — use your hands — then add the cheese and mix it thoroughly along with the salt and cayenne pepper. Gently combine with the cereal. Shape into balls. Place them on a buttered cookie sheet and flatten them slightly. Put a nut or a very small square of cheese on top as a trimming. Bake in a 300°F oven for 10 to 12 minutes. Be careful not to let them burn; they should be cheese coloured, not brown.

BELLE'S CHEESE COOKIES

These have a nippy crispness that makes you eat more and more.

¼ cup soft butter
¼ teaspoon salt
Pinch of cayenne pepper
1 cup grated sharp Cheddar cheese
½ cup crushed Rice Krispies
½ cup flour

Mix thoroughly, shape into balls, and put them on a buttered cookie sheet and flatten with a fork. Bake at 375°F for 8 to 10 minutes.

CHEESE TRUFFLES

Sue Antonello brought these to a Beta Sigma Phi chapter meeting one night; they were soon gobbled up.

2 cups shredded Cheddar cheese
½ cup cream cheese
¼ cup softened butter
¼ cup sherry
1 teaspoon grated lemon rind
¼ teaspoon dry mustard
¼ teaspoon nutmeg
1½ cups finely chopped almonds

Combine all of the ingredients except the almonds in a food processor. Refrigerate until firm, then make bite-sized balls and roll in almond crumbs. You should have 50 to 60 balls — you'll need all of them.

SQUARES

Faster to make than cookies because you don't have any rolling or dropping from a spoon, squares are usually richer and stickier, and can often be cut large enough for a dessert. They are a great invention, and Eva has told me they are becoming even more popular than pies in her Mennonite community.

OATMEAL CHOCOLATE SQUARES

Sheila Hutton says this is an easy one to make for a party.

1 cup butter or margarine
¼ cup white sugar
⅔ cup brown sugar
3 cups rolled oats
⅛ cup chocolate chips
¾ cup peanut butter

Melt the butter, add the sugars, and then the rolled oats; press into a large, ungreased pan. Bake for 15 minutes at 350°F and cool in the pan. Melt the chocolate chips and peanut butter together, spread on top of the baked mixture, and refrigerate until firm. Cut into squares.

LIZZIE FREY'S CHOCODILLOS

Lizzie warns, "You chust can't stop eating these once you start."

½ cup butter or margarine
½ cup shortening, lard, or margarine
⅓ cup crunchy peanut butter
1¼ cups brown sugar
¼ teaspoon salt
1 egg
1 teaspoon vanilla
2½ cups flour

Topping:
1 cup chocolate chips
½ cup crunchy peanut butter
½ cup desiccated coconut

Blend butter, shortening, peanut butter, sugar, salt, egg, and vanilla. Add flour and mix thoroughly. Press the mixture firmly into an unbuttered 10" x 15" pan. Bake at 350°F for about 25 minutes. Meanwhile, melt the chocolate chips. Stir in the peanut butter and coconut. Spread the topping over the warm baked base in the pan. Let cool. Cut into bars or squares. You'll have a lot, but they won't last long.

NORM'S CHOCOLATE SQUARES

I made these for our Cress family reunion, and everyone said, "Good."

½ cup brown sugar
½ cup butter
1 cup flour

Topping:
1 cup brown sugar
3 tablespoons cocoa
2 tablespoons flour
½ teaspoon salt
1 teaspoon baking powder
2 eggs, beaten
¾ cup chopped nuts
1 teaspoon vanilla

Combine ½ cup brown sugar, butter, and 1 cup flour, and pack into a 9" x 9" pan. To make the topping, mix 1 cup sugar, cocoa, 2 tablespoons flour, salt, and baking powder. Stir in the eggs, nuts, and vanilla, and mix well. Spread topping over the base and bake at 325°F for about 35 minutes. Cut into squares.
They freeze well.

BUTTERSCOTCH SQUARES

Chewy and buttery — Norm makes these often.

¼ cup butter
1 cup brown sugar
1 egg
¾ cup flour
1 teaspoon baking powder
1¼ teaspoons vanilla
½ cup nuts

Cook butter and sugar till well blended. Cool to lukewarm and add unbeaten egg; beat well. Add flour and baking powder, then vanilla and nuts. Spread the dough on a greased pan, bake 25 minutes in a 350°F oven, then cut into squares.

PECAN SQUARES

To be at their best, squares should be eaten when they are fresh. That is usually no problem. But if you can't manage a whole panful at a sitting, you can freeze what is left and enjoy them again.

¼ cup butter
⅓ cup brown sugar
1 cup flour
¼ teaspoon baking powder
½ cup finely chopped pecans

Topping:
2 eggs
¾ cup dark corn syrup
⅓ cup brown sugar
3 tablespoons flour
½ teaspoon salt
1 teaspoon vanilla
1 cup coarsely broken pecans

Combine first five ingredients. Work mixture until crumbly. Press into a lightly greased 8" x 11" or 8" x 12" pan. Bake 10 minutes at 350°F. Meantime, beat eggs well and add corn syrup, brown sugar, flour, salt, vanilla, and pecans. Spread over base and bake at 350°F for 30 minutes or until light brown.

JEAN SALTER'S CRUNCHY OAT SQUARES

Crisp, great flavour, and not too sweet.

⅔ cup packed brown sugar
½ cup butter
½ cup margarine
¼ teaspoon salt
3 tablespoons corn syrup
1 tablespoon lemon juice
2⅓ cups rolled oats
2⅓ cups wheat flakes (or rolled oats)

Put sugar, butter, margarine, salt, and syrup into a pan and heat until sugar is dissolved. Add lemon juice. Cool slightly and stir in the rolled oats and wheat flakes. (You could use all oats if you don't have any wheat flakes.) Pack the mixture on a greased cookie sheet or roasting pan and bake in a 350°F oven for about 20 to 30 minutes. Watch them. When golden, leave to cool then chill before cutting into squares or bars.

You may have a small dishful of crumbs after you've cut them; they make a good topping for ice cream or yoghurt.

CHOCOLATE ORANGE BARS

This is a great combination.

⅓ cup soft butter
½ cup brown sugar
2 egg yolks
1 tablespoon grated orange rind
1¼ cup flour
1 teaspoon baking powder
¼ teaspoon salt
⅓ cup orange juice

Topping:
½ cup chocolate chips
¼ cup chopped walnuts
2 egg whites
¾ cup brown sugar

Beat the butter, ½ cup brown sugar, and egg yolks together until fluffy. Stir in the orange rind. Sift the flour, baking powder, and salt together and add to the first mixture alternately with the orange juice. Turn the batter into a buttered pan and spread evenly. Sprinkle with chocolate chips and walnuts. Beat the egg whites until fluffy, add ¾ cup brown sugar gradually, and keep beating until stiff and glossy. Spread over the other layers in the pan. Bake about 35 minutes in a 325°F oven, or until the meringue is golden and dry to the touch. Cool in the pan and cut into squares or bars. Then eat it; don't let it sit around till the meringue looks stale.

LEBKUCHEN

Fruity, cakey squares, improved by a bit of icing.

¼ cup shortening
½ cup brown sugar
1 egg, beaten
½ cup molasses
½ teaspoon baking soda
½ cup hot coffee
2 cups flour
1 tablespoon cocoa
½ teaspoon cinnamon
½ teaspoon cloves
½ teaspoon allspice
½ teaspoon salt
½ pound mixed peel
½ cup chopped nuts
Butter icing

Cream the shortening and sugar, add egg, and mix well. Add molasses; dissolve soda in hot coffee and add. Sift flour and cocoa with spices and salt and stir into the first mixture alternately with mixed peel and nuts. Grease a large cookie sheet; spread the batter to a ½ inch thickness on the sheet, allowing for spreading. Bake in a 350°F oven for 20 minutes. Cool, ice with soft butter icing, and cut into squares. You could ice the squares all around with a butter icing moistened with strong coffee or cocoa.

PEANUT BUTTER SQUARES

When I called in at Eva's house after going to the market one Saturday, she immediately brought out two large panfuls of squares and cut a generous piece for me to sample. Next day I gave the recipe to my sister Norm, who could hardly wait to get at it. Just read it over and try to restrain yourself. It's quick and easy and makes a lot. Eva said sometimes she uses margarine instead of butter, and the men don't know the difference — but she does.

½ cup butter or margarine
1 cup brown sugar
½ cup corn syrup
2 teaspoons vanilla
1 teaspoon salt
4 cups rolled oats
Peanut butter
1 cup or more chocolate chips

Cream butter and sugar. Add corn syrup, vanilla, salt, and rolled oats. Mix well, then spread in a 9" x 13" pan and bake at 350°F for about 15 minutes. When slightly cool, slather with peanut butter — as thick or thin as you like. Sprinkle with chocolate chips and press them into the peanut butter or — as Norm did — put the pan back into the oven just long enough to melt the chips slightly so they'll stick when they're cold. Cut into squares when cool.

These are truly scrumptious. They'd be good, too, without peanut butter if you don't like it.

CORN FLAKE DREAM BARS

Norm says these are Jim's favourites. Jim is her handsome bachelor son.

¼ cup butter
½ cup brown sugar
1 cup flour

Topping:
2 eggs
1 cup brown sugar
1 cup corn flakes
1 cup coconut
1 teaspoon vanilla
½ cup chopped walnuts
Salt

Mix the first three ingredients and pack in a square pan. Mix topping ingredients in order given. Pour topping over base and bake about 15 minutes at 350°F, until golden or light brown. If you bake them too long, they are dry.

SESAME SQUARES

These have a nutty, chewy flavour with a meringue-like top, which may crack when you cut the squares, but don't let that stop you.

Bottom layer:
½ cup brown sugar
½ cup margarine or butter
1¼ cups flour

Top layer:
¾ cup brown sugar
2 tablespoons flour
⅔ teaspoon baking powder
1 egg
½ teaspoon vanilla
½ teaspoon almond flavouring
½ cup sesame seeds

Cream bottom-layer ingredients together till smooth, then pat into a 9" x 9" ungreased pan and bake at 350°F for 15 minutes. Blend top-layer ingredients together and pour over the baked layer. Return to the oven and bake at 350°F for 15 minutes. While still warm, cut into squares.

PECAN FINGERS

Hannah told me that all the ladies at her quilting for Magdalene wanted this recipe.

1 cup dark brown sugar
1 cup soft butter
1 egg
1 teaspoon vanilla
2 cups flour

Topping:
1 egg, beaten
1 cup dark brown sugar
1 cup coarsely chopped pecans

Cream 1 cup brown sugar and butter until fluffy. Add 1 egg and vanilla and blend well. Stir the flour into the creamed mixture, working until well blended. Spread in a buttered cake pan. Brush with 1 beaten egg. Sprinkle ½ cup brown sugar over it, then sprinkle the nuts over that, then the other ½ cup brown sugar — as evenly as you can. Don't let any part be uncovered. Bake in a 350°F oven for 20 to 25 minutes, until nicely golden. Cool in the pan then cut into fingers to serve. Hannah says dark brown sugar gives the best flavour but any brown sugar will do. Good luck.

JEAN SALTER'S RAISIN MUMBLES

With a name like that, how could they be anything but great?

Filling:
2½ cups raisins
½ cup sugar
2 cups water
1 tablespoon lemon juice
2 tablespoons cornstarch

Cook all but the cornstarch over a low heat for about 30 minutes, then thicken with the cornstarch dissolved in very little water.

Top and bottom:
¾ cup soft butter
1 cup dark brown sugar
1¾ cups flour
½ teaspoon salt
½ teaspoon baking soda
1½ cups rolled oats

Mix together and divide into two. Press half into a buttered baking tin, pour on the raisin filling, then top with the remainder. Bake in a 400°F oven for 20 to 30 minutes. Cool and cut into squares.

GRANOLA BARS

Kae Hobson loves these — and so do her grandchildren.

> **2 cups dessicated coconut, or less**
> **1½ cups rolled oats**
> **1½ cups raisins**
> **2 cups sunflower seeds**
> **½ cup sesame seeds**
> **¾ cup peanuts**
> **½ cup dried fruit — apricots, prunes,**
> **apples, etc. (optional)**
> **½ teaspoon salt**
> **1 cup liquid honey**
> **1 teaspoon vanilla**
> **½ cup peanut butter, or more**

Mix all the dry ingredients; thoroughly blend the honey, vanilla, and peanut butter. Grease your hands and mix the whole works really well. If you want thick bars, put everything into a 9" x 12" pan, pressing down with a heated spoon. If you want thin, crisp bars, spread the mixture on well-buttered cookie sheets and press down. Bake at 275°F for 12 minutes or till golden. Cool the pans on a rack and cut with a hot knife. I defy you to stop after eating one bar.

SHOO-FLY SQUARES

When the ladies of the big Anglican church in Galt — now Cambridge — had a money-raising luncheon, the recipes they used came from *Food that Really Schmecks*. To make the use of dessert plates and forks unnecessary, they baked the Shoo-fly Pie with a wet bottom in large sheets that could be cut into squares and eaten with one's fingers.

> **Pastry for a 9-inch cake pan**
>
> *Bottom part:*
> **¾ cup boiling water**
> **½ teaspoon baking soda**
> **1 cup molasses**

Top part:
1½ cups flour
1 cup brown sugar
¾ cup shortening
¼ teaspoon salt

Pour boiling water over soda in a bowl and stir in the molasses.
Pour into the pastry-lined cake pan. Mix ingredients for the top
part and sprinkle over the molasses mixture. Bake in a 350°F
oven for 30 to 40 minutes. Let cool and cut into squares.

HANNAH'S MAPLE SQUARES

One Saturday morning when Hannah and I were having a cup
of tea at her kitchen table, her ever-smiling, pretty daughter
Ruth tempted us beyond endurance with a plate full of fresh-
baked Maple Squares.

Bottom:
1 cup flour
¼ cup brown sugar
½ cup butter

Top:
⅔ cup brown sugar
1 cup maple syrup
2 eggs, beaten
¼ cup softened butter
¼ teaspoon salt
½ teaspoon vanilla
2 tablespoons flour
⅔ cup nuts or raisins

For bottom: Rub flour, sugar, and butter together, then press
into a square or 7" x 11" pan. Bake in a 350°F oven for 5 minutes.

For top: Combine the brown sugar and syrup in a saucepan
and simmer for 5 minutes. Cool before pouring over beaten eggs,
stirring all the time. Add the remaining ingredients and spread
over partially baked base. Bake at 350°F for 30 minutes or until
golden. Cool and cut into squares — not too large. They are
very rich, but delicious.

BUTTER TART BARS

Pat Bourke, a *Schmecks* fan from Toronto, sent me this recipe, which she thinks is wonderful. So do I — so will you.

¾ cup flour
¼ cup brown sugar
⅓ cup butter

Topping:
1 cup raisins
2 eggs
½ cup sugar
½ cup corn syrup
⅛ teaspoon salt
1 teaspoon vanilla
¼ cup flour

Blend ¾ cup flour, brown sugar, and butter until crumbly; press into buttered 8" x 8" ungreased pan. Bake at 350°F for 12 to 15 minutes.

Cover raisins with boiling water. When soft, drain. Beat eggs and gradually beat in sugar. Add corn syrup, salt, vanilla, and flour. Beat well. Stir in raisins. Pour over baked layer. Bake at 350°F for 25 to 30 minutes until topping is golden. Cool and cut into bars or squares.

BEVVY'S BUTTERNUT SQUARES

Have you seen any butternuts lately? When we were kids, Daddy used to take us into the country, stop our Briscoe at the side of a bush, and we'd wander around till we came to a butternut tree with sticky green nuts lying under it. At home we'd spread the nuts on papers in the attic till the sticky green shells became hard and dry, then Daddy would open them for us with a hammer. (For these squares, I now use pecans.)

1 cup dark brown sugar
1 cup butter
1 egg, well beaten
2 cups flour

Topping:
1 egg, well beaten
½ cup dark brown sugar
1 cup coarsely chopped nuts

Cream the sugar and butter, add the egg, and mix well. Work in the flour gradually, then spread the mixture in a thin layer on a greased baking sheet. For the topping, brush on the well-beaten egg; sprinkle ¼ cup of the brown sugar over it, then the chopped nuts and the rest of the sugar. Bake in a 350°F oven for 20 to 25 minutes. Cut into squares when slightly cooled.

RICH AND GOOEY NUT SQUARES

Lucky is the girl who takes these to a box social; they attract young men like flies.

⅓ cup butter
½ cup brown sugar
1⅓ cups flour
1 teaspoon baking powder
¼ cup finely chopped nuts

Cream the butter and brown sugar, add the flour and baking powder, sifted together, and then stir in the chopped nuts. Pat firmly into a 9" x 9" pan and bake at 350°F for 7 minutes only. No longer. Remove from the oven.
    Meanwhile, you could be stirring up:

2 eggs
¾ cup corn syrup
¼ cup brown sugar
½ teaspoon salt
1 teaspoon vanilla
3 tablespoons flour
¾ cup coarsely chopped nuts

Beat the eggs until foamy and add the corn syrup, sugar, salt, vanilla, and flour. Mix well and pour over the baked part. Sprinkle the chopped nuts on top and bake at 350°F for about 15 minutes. Do not overbake. Cut into squares while warm.

BONNIE BENNETT'S SQUARES

Bonnie lives at the top of the hill on our road and she often brings me her favourite creations.

> 1 cup butter
> 1 cup brown sugar
> 1 teaspoon vanilla
> 2 cups flour
> 1 cup chocolate chips
> 1 cup walnuts

Mix all the ingredients and press them into a 9" x 9" unbuttered pan. Bake in a 350°F oven for about 25 minutes, or till they are golden. While they are still warm, cut into squares or bars and take some to share with your neighbour.

DATE SQUARES

You never get tired of this old favourite.

> 1 cup butter
> 1 cup or less brown sugar
> 1½ cups flour
> 1 teaspoon baking powder
> ¼ teaspoon salt
> 1½ cups rolled oats
> ¼ cup chopped walnuts (optional)
> Date filling (see page 59)

Cream butter and sugar; add flour, baking powder, and salt, sifted together, then add the oats and nuts. Pat half the crumbly mixture into the bottom of a greased square pan, spread the date filling over it, and cover with the remaining oat mixture. Or distribute the mixture and filling in several layers, topping with oat mixture. Bake in a 350°F oven for about 45 minutes.

These squares, loaded with delicious calories, are a complete dessert, topped with whipped or ice cream. You might try them with different fillings — jam or raisins, instead of dates; Bevvy says ground cherries are good, too.

DATE AND ORANGE SQUARES

These taste even better than old-fashioned date squares and are easier and quicker to make if you have a blender or food processor.

Filling:
1½ cups pitted dates
¾ cup sugar
Rind of 1 orange
1½ cups boiling water (or half orange juice)
½ to 1 cup chopped pecans (optional)

Put the dates, sugar, orange rind, and boiling water into the blender or food processor and whirl until it is like soft jam. Stir in the chopped pecans. (If you don't have a blender, all is not lost: you must chop the dates, grate the orange rind, and gently cook them with the sugar and water to a jam-like consistency before adding the nuts.)

Top and bottom:
1 cup butter
1¼ cups brown sugar
1½ cups flour
1 teaspoon baking powder
½ teaspoon salt
1½ cups rolled oats

Cream the butter and brown sugar together; add the flour, baking powder, and salt, sifted together, then the oats; mix until crumbly. Pat half the mixture into the bottom of a buttered 9" x 9" pan. Spread the date filling over it, then cover with the remaining oat mixture. Bake in a 325°F oven for 45 minutes, but watch it. Serve warm or cold. With or without whipped or ice cream, it is a fabulous dessert.

RASPBERRY BARS

Norm and Ralph have a raspberry patch in their garden — and lots of raspberry jam.

1 cup softened butter
⅓ cup sugar
2 egg yolks
2 cups flour
1 cup raspberry jam
4 tablespoons sugar
½ cup chopped nuts

Cream the butter and ⅓ cup sugar. Beat in the egg yolks; stir in the flour ½ cup at a time. Press half the mixture into a 9" x 9" pan. Spread with jam and top with the rest of the dough. Sprinkle with 4 tablespoons sugar and nuts. Bake at 375°F for 25 minutes.

CRANBERRY CHEWS

On her file card with this recipe Lorna has written, "delicious."

1½ cups flour
2 tablespoons sugar
¼ teaspoon salt
½ cup butter

Combine until the mixture is crumbly, then press evenly into a 9" x 9" Pyrex pan and bake at 350°F for 10 minutes.

1½ to 2 cups cranberry sauce

Spread evenly over the baked layer.

2 eggs
1½ cups firmly packed brown sugar
2 tablespoons flour
1 teaspoon vanilla
¾ cup coconut
½ cup coarsely chopped pecans or filberts
1 cup wheat flakes

Beat the eggs with the brown sugar, flour, and vanilla until fluffy. Stir in the coconut and nuts. Spread over the cranberry layer; sprinkle with the wheat flakes. Bake 30 minutes at 350°F, or until the topping is firm. Cool in the pan and cut into bars. These will make any party plate look festive.

CHEERY CHERRY BARS

A great thing to do with the cherries you froze last summer — or fresh ones. Romance blossoms when these appear at an Old Order Mennonite Singing.

Mix and pat into a buttered 9" x 9" cake pan:

1 cup flour
¼ cup white or brown sugar
½ cup butter

Bake for 10 minutes at 350°F while you mix together:

1 cup brown sugar
¼ teaspoon salt
½ teaspoon baking powder
¼ cup flour
2 eggs, lightly beaten

Fold in:
⅓ cup coconut
1 cup or more cherries
½ cup walnuts

Spread the mixture over the half-baked dough in the pan and bake at 325°F for about 30 minutes, till golden. Cut into bars when cool. If you want to be fancy, you may ice by blending:

1 cup brown sugar
1 tablespoon milk or cherry juice
¼ cup table cream
Icing sugar

Boil 2 minutes, let cool, and add enough icing sugar to thicken. These will be a hit when you serve them. Don't try to keep them; they should be eaten fresh.

PLUM CUSTARD KUCHEN

A tea-biscuit base with neat rows of plums surrounded by custard — this is an intriguing and delicious dessert. The last time I made it I ran out of plums and filled in the spaces with frozen cherries.

1⅓ cups flour
¼ teaspoon baking powder
1 teaspoon salt
2 tablespoons sugar
⅓ cup margarine or shortening
1 egg, beaten
1 cup milk
Plums, pitted and halved

Topping:
½ cup sugar
1 teaspoon cinnamon

Custard:
1 egg, beaten
½ cup sour cream
½ cup buttermilk or yoghurt
⅓ cup sugar

Sift together flour, baking powder, salt, and sugar. Cut in margarine. Add egg and milk and stir into mixture. Pat the dough into the bottom of a 9" x 9" cake pan. Arrange nicely in rows enough pitted plums to completely cover the dough. Sprinkle topping over the plums. Bake at 400°F for 15 minutes.

Meanwhile, mix custard ingredients. Take the kuchen out of the oven, drizzle the custard mixture over the plums, and return it to the oven. Reduce heat to 350°F and bake for another 30 minutes. Serve warm.

PLATZ

When Rudy Wiebe came to the Provident Bookstore in Kitchener to autograph his latest novel, they served coffee and Platz, a Russian Mennonite fruit coffee cake. It was so popular that I asked Gloria Dirks for her recipe.

1½ cups flour
1 tablespoon baking powder
1 teaspoon sugar
½ teaspoon salt
½ cup butter or margarine
½ cup table cream or whole milk

Topping:
Fruit, in sections: plums, apples, apricots,
    or peaches
1 cup sugar
½ cup flour
3 tablespoons butter

Sift together the 1½ cups flour, baking powder, 1 teaspoon sugar, and salt. Cut in the butter as you would for pastry; blend in the cream. Pat out the dough into a greased 9" x 9" pan. Place fruit sections side by side on the dough and sprinkle with the crumbs made by blending together the 1 cup sugar, ½ cup flour, and butter. Bake at 350°F till golden. Cut into squares. (At the bookstore, the Platz had a single piece of fruit placed neatly in the centre of each square.)

CHEWY BROWNIES

The best I've ever tasted.

½ cup butter
1 cup brown sugar
1 egg
½ cup cocoa
1 cup walnuts
1 teaspoon vanilla
½ cup flour
Pinch of salt

Mix the ingredients in the order given and bake at 350°F for 20 minutes in a greased cake pan. The brownies, cut into squares, will be soft and seem to be not finished — but that's the secret of their fudginess. They never get stale — at Norm's house they are often eaten before they have a chance to get cold.

If you want the brownies even more chocolately, use 2 squares of melted unsweetened chocolate instead of cocoa.

BLONDE BROWNIES

Caroline Haehnel makes these using sunflower seeds instead of nuts — less expensive and no bother chopping. They taste as good or better, she says.

>⅓ cup vegetable oil
>1½ cups brown sugar
>2 eggs, beaten
>1 teaspoon vanilla
>1 cup flour
>1 teaspoon baking powder
>½ teaspoon salt
>1 cup toasted sunflower seeds or chopped nuts
>½ cup chocolate chips

Blend the oil, sugar, eggs, and vanilla. Sift the flour, baking powder, and salt into the oil mixture and blend well. Stir in the seeds and chips, or sprinkle the chocolate chips on top after you have spread the batter in a buttered 9" x 9" pan. Bake at 350°F for about 30 minutes, or until the top springs back when touched lightly. Cool and cut into bars. These may be iced if you want to gild the lily.

MOIST AND MORE-ISH BROWNIES

Norm has tried many brownie recipes in her life, and I agree with her that this is one of the best. We like them moist, not dry or crumbly.

>½ cup butter
>4 eggs, beaten till light
>¼ teaspoon salt
>2 cups sugar
>4 squares unsweetened chocolate, melted
>   and cooled, or ½ cup cocoa
>1 teaspoon vanilla
>1 cup flour
>1 cup chopped walnuts

Cream the butter; add beaten eggs and salt, and then add the sugar gradually. Keep beating until the mixture is light and creamy. Fold in the chocolate and vanilla. Sift and add the flour, beating the batter until smooth. Fold in walnuts. Spread in a buttered 9" x 9" pan and bake at 325°F for about 30 minutes. Wait until they cool before you eat them.

KIT'S JAM BARS

When Kit came to Sunfish for lunch one day, she brought a panful of these easy-to-make, not-too-rich but delicious jam bars or squares. I ate one, I ate two, I ate three, then I quit — but I repeated my performance four hours later, and again the next day — until there were none.

> ½ **cup butter or margarine at room temperature**
> ½ **cup brown sugar**
> 1 **cup flour**
> ¼ **teaspoon baking soda**
> ⅛ **teaspoon salt**
> 1 **cup rolled oats**
> ¾ **cup jam or marmalade (Kit used marmalade and**
> **strawberry jam)**

Blend all the ingredients except the jam. Press 2 cups of the mixture into a buttered 8" x 8" pan, then slather it with the jam to within ¼ inch of the edges. Cover with the rest of the oat mixture and bake in a 350°F oven for 35 to 40 minutes. Cut into bars or squares before cooled.

INDEX